Marx 200
– a review of Marx's economics
200 years after his birth

Marx 200

– a review of Marx's economics 200 years after his birth

© Michael Roberts 2018
Graphic design: Eva Kinch Hall, Ordered by Colour
Published and printed by Lulu.com
Printed in London, UK 2018

ISBN: 978-0-244-07625-2

Marx 200

– a review of Marx's economics
200 years after his birth

Michael Roberts

Contents

Marx 200

This short book concentrates on explaining Marx's economic ideas and their relevance to modern economies 200 years after his birth. Marx developed three key laws of motion of capitalism, around which a clear analysis of the nature of modern economies can be understood.

From these laws, we can understand why capitalism cannot escape being subject to regular and recurring slumps; causes vicious rivalry among national states that leads to perpetual wars; and engenders uncontrolled and wasteful use of natural resources that now threatens the destruction of the planet itself.

Marx's laws also tell us that capitalism is not here for eternity but has a finite existence. The question before us, 200 years after Marx's birth, is what would replace it as a mode of production and social organisation for human beings on this planet.

The development of Marx's economic thought can be divided into four parts: his childhood; as a young man; as a mature man; and the old Marx.

In his teenage years, he was under the influence of his father and his father's friend, Count Von Westphalen. They were both men of the enlightenment, followers of the ideals of the French philosophers and revolution. Marx was born just after the end of the so-called Napoleonic wars and at the start of a gradual economic recovery in the petty German statelets. When Marx went to university in the late 1830s, he was a radical democrat in opinion, one of the 'Young Hegelians', who were philosophically opposed to religious superstition and autocracy.

The period of Marx as a young man from the point of him leaving university and without an academic post was one of radical upsurge in ideas and political action in Europe. Britain was in the midst of the 'industrial revolution' with all its expansion of machinery and goods and the accompanying dark exploitation of labour. The Reform Act of 1832 had given the middle classes the vote but now there was pressure from the Chartist working class movement for full franchise. In

Germany, workers in the towns were organising for the first time and peasants in country were growing restive. Economically, in 1840 there was the establishment of the German Customs Union, the Zollverein, which brought an end to trade barriers within the Prussian sphere of influence and began a huge economic upsurge.

On leaving university, Marx became a radical journalist with a growing materialist conception of class struggle. Marx started to take an interest in economic developments under the encouragement of his new and eventually lifetime friend, Friedrich Engels. Engels lived in the heart of Capital, Britain's industrial Manchester, and was already writing on the economic and social consequences of capitalist development. Marx and Engels became communists, an ideology designed to replace capitalism as a mode of production and social organisation with communal control, with the working class as the 'gravediggers' of capitalism to deliver this. They wrote the Communist Manifesto in March 1848, just before the outbreak of the revolutions against autocracy across Europe. The manifesto intuitively recognised the nature of capitalism, but without expounding any economic laws of motion.

The defeat of the 1848 revolutions and Marx's eventual exile to Britain began the period of mature Marx (aged 32) that lasted until the defeat of the Paris Commune in 1871 (aged 53). This turned out to be the period of the long boom in the European economies. Britain was the dominant economic and political power and thus the best placed to study the economics of capitalism. The boom revealed to Marx and Engels that there was no short cut to revolution and capitalism still had some way to go in its spread across the globe. The first international slump in 1857 did not lead to the collapse of capitalism or to revolution. Marx concentrated on organising the first international party of the working class (the International Working Men's Association) and on writing his main economic work, Capital.

The defeat of the Paris Commune in 1871, followed by the financial panic and crash of 1873 in the US, which spread to Europe, set the final phase of Marx's life. It was also the start of what was eventually called the (first) Great Depression, where the major capitalist economies struggled to recover from crashes and became subject to a series of slumps. This was a vindication of Marx's laws of motion. Marx died in 1883, in the depth of the latest slump in Britain.

Marx remained an obscure figure in economic and political thought after his death, except in the circles of the leaders of the burgeoning social democratic parties of Europe after the Great Depression came to an end. In this new period of economic recovery of the 1890s, unskilled workers formed trade unions and working class organisations built mass political parties with increasing voting power. Marx's ideas now became more widespread. The victory of the 'Bolshevik' (majority) social democrats in the Russian revolution in 1917 then placed the works of Marx and Engels on the world stage through the 20th century.

This book will look back at Marx's economic ideas and see just how relevant they are for 21st century.

CHAPTER ONE

Marx's economics

Karl Heinrich Marx was born in Trier, Germany, which was part of the Prussian monarchical state. Marx was from a Jewish family that converted to Protestantism during his childhood. His childhood sweetheart was Jenny Von Westphalen (whom he was later to marry). She was the daughter of the local squire or aristocrat, Count von Westphalen. He and Marx's father were friends, as both were influenced by the enlightenment ideas purveying France and Germany at that time. Karl got his initial liberal leanings from the discussions and books provided by the two. Marx's birthplace was in Bruckenstrasse 10, in Trier. The family

Marx's birthplace in Trier

occupied two rooms on the ground floor and three on the first floor. It was purchased by the Social Democratic Party of Germany in 1928 and it now houses a museum devoted to him.

Marx studied philosophy in the Universities of Bonn, Berlin and Jena from where he gained a doctorate in philosophy at the age of 23. As a student, he was involved in circles of young philosophers known as the Young Hegelians. He worked as a journalist and editor for the influential newspaper Rheinische Zeitung of Cologne. At this time, he was a radical liberal, not a socialist. But the radical perspective of the newspaper led the Prussian authorities initially to censor and later close down the newspaper and to the exile of Marx. He took refuge in France and settled in Paris, where he had the opportunity to study French utopian socialism. He became a communist, as it was called.

Young Marx

Friedrich Engels, his close friend, collaborator and financial supporter, was the son of a German industrialist. On the one hand, Engels occupied himself with the business activities of his family, assuming the responsibility of the operation of a factory in Manchester, England, and, on the other hand, being an intellectual, he published significant works and was involved in the socialist movement. He met with Marx in Paris in 1844, while he was visiting for a short trip. Thus began a lifelong friendship and joint work.

Engels and Marx became involved in what was eventually called the Communist League, a body of semi-secret workers based across Europe. They were commissioned to write the manifesto of the group which was published in early 1848 just before the outbreak of revolutions against the authoritarian semi-feudal monarchies in Europe. In the Manifesto of the Communist Party, written 170 years ago, Marx developed a startling new economic perception of the nature of capitalism, the new and growing mode of production in human society.

"The need of a constantly expanding market for its products chases the bourgeoisie over the entire surface of the globe. It must nestle everywhere, settle everywhere, establish connexions everywhere. Modern bourgeois society, with its relations of production, of exchange and of property, a society that has conjured up such gigantic means of production and of exchange, is like the sorcerer who is no longer able to control the powers of the nether world whom he has called up by his spells. It is enough to mention the commercial crises that by their periodical return put the existence of the entire bourgeois society on its trial, each time more threateningly. In these crises, a great part not only of the existing products, but also of the previously created productive forces, is periodically destroyed. In these crises, there breaks out an epidemic that, in all earlier epochs, would have seemed an absurdity — the epidemic of over-production. And how does the bourgeoisie get over these crises? On the one hand, by enforced destruction of a mass of productive forces; on the other, by the conquest of new markets, and by the more thorough exploitation of the old ones. That is to say, by paving the way for more extensive and more destructive crises, and by diminishing the means whereby crises are prevented."
Communist Manifesto 1848.

The mature Marx in England

In the Manifesto, Marx had seen how capitalism would develop but he had not yet worked out the mechanics and laws of motion of capitalist development. It was Engels who encouraged Marx to study the works of the English classical economists. With the collapse and defeat of the 1848 revolutions, Marx was forced into exile eventually to England. And amid poverty and family illness, he began to study economics (or what was called political economy then) deeply for the first time.

Throughout the 1850s, he worked in the British Museum and compiled detailed notes on the theories of the so-called classical economists of the early 19th century, Adam Smith, David Ricardo, James Mill, Thomas Malthus and many others. It was then that he developed his three great laws of motion of capitalism: the law of value, the law of accumulation and the law of profitability. From these laws, Marx's theory of crises under capitalism can be derived. The laws also explain why capitalism is a mode of production that would be exhausted in its ability to increase the 'productive forces' of human society and would have to be replaced.

These laws were expounded in Marx's notes on economics (Grundrisse) and in his plan of books on Capital (a project that he never finished). By 1857, Marx had accumulated over 800 pages of notes and short essays on capital, landed property, wage labour, the state and foreign trade and the world market.

The Panic of 1857 was the first international crisis of industrial capitalism and signalled that Marx and Engels were right about this new mode of production being subject to regular crises. In the second half of 1857 and in the first three months of 1858, Marx made a significant and important change to his working method. He did not go to the library of the British Museum, but turned his modest study room into an analysis centre: *"I am working enormously, as a rule until 4 o'clock in the morning. The work is, in fact, a double one: 1. Elaborating the outlines of political economy ["so that I at least understand the groundwork before the déluge"] 2. The present crisis. Apart from the articles for the Tribune, all I do is keep records of it, which, however, takes up considerable amount of time."* [1]

Marx was optimistic that his empirical studies of the 1857 crisis would confirm his developing theory of crises. Marx began his research for the Book of the Crisis of 1857 with the preparation of bankruptcy data, which he had collected before the section on the money market. In the third Book of the Commercial Crisis, Marx integrated the bankruptcy data into the money market section. Unfortunately, Marx began his research on the Bank of England monetary data too late. So, contrary to his expectations, he did not document the worsening of the financial crisis.

According to Marx's theory of crises, the financial crisis should be followed by an industrial crisis. It seemed to him that Engels, who wrote to him on 11 December, had also confirmed this idea: *"Never before has overproduction been so general as during the present crisis."* So Marx

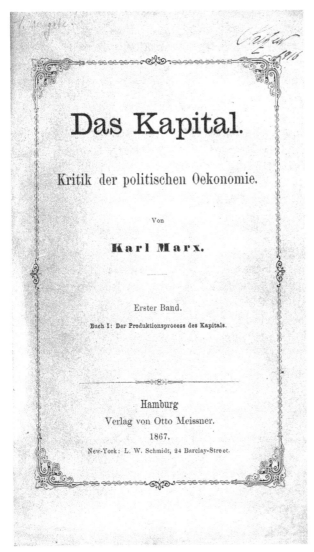

The first edition of Capital, 1867

systematically collected price data from the Economist for both the cotton industry's raw materials and its finished products. And he collected excerpts from The Manchester Guardian, gathering information about the workers and factories in Manchester and Salford affected by partial work hours.

But Marx's empirical data was just inadequate and too untimely to help him understand exactly how the 1857-8 economic slump started and finished. But it did show to him that crises would appear but not necessarily lead to revolution. The connection between crises and revolution was much more complicated.

In 1859, Marx published A Contribution to the Critique of Political Economy, his first serious economic work. This work was intended as a preview of Das Kapital (English title: Capital: Critique of Political Economy), which he intended to publish at a later date. But it took another eight years (interrupted by the need to make a living, illness and deaths in the family and revolutionary work) before Capital Volume One was published in 1867. Subsequently, Marx spent time on revising this for new editions (the French in 1872) but never got round to completing manuscripts for the rest of the work. It was left to Engels after Marx's death in 1883 to edit Marx's inexorable and obscure writing in order to publish Volumes Two and Three of Capital (1894), while his Theories of Surplus Value (often considered as Volume Four), first written in the 1850s, was edited and published by Karl Kautsky, the German Marxist leader, in 1905, although much of these volumes did not appear in English for many decades.

Marx never stopped trying to back up his laws of motion of capitalism and his theory of crises with empirical evidence. Indeed, Marx, the empirical researcher, dealt with seven successive cycles in his lifetime.[2] In a letter to Engels in May 1873, Marx wrote: *'I have just sent Moore a history which privatim had to be smuggled in. But he thinks that the question is unsolvable or at least pro tempore unsolvable in view of the many parts in which facts are still to be discovered relating to this question. The matter is as follows: you know tables in which prices, calculated by percent etc., etc. are represented in their growth in the course of a year are showing the increases and decreases by zig-zag lines. I have repeatedly attempted, for the analysis of crises, to compute these "ups and downs" as fictional curves, and I thought (and even now I still think this possible with sufficient empirical material) to infer mathematically from this an important law of crises. Moore, as I already said, considers the problem rather impractical, and I have decided for the time being to give it up.'*[3]

In his later years, Marx concentrated on analysing the role of credit in crises and how they were connected to the regular crises in production.

Much of this research has only just been published in English from Marx's notes in the MEGA project.

Marx's great economic discovery of the 1850s and his major contribution to political economy was how the capitalist mode of production extracted value from human labour. Primitive communism had no concept of exploitation because all produce was gathered by common labour and distributed commonly. There was no surplus over basic needs because the level of productivity of labour was so low. Communism was by necessity. But, with the development of technology and increased productivity from farming crops and livestock, a surplus over and above basic needs became possible. And with a surplus came the opportunity by arms, by religious magic and expertise, for an elite to control that surplus.

Surplus labour became the province of the elite (or ruling class) in ancient slave societies, medieval feudal Europe and Asian bureaucratic empires.

The history of human society has been the history of exploitation and the control of surplus labour and the class struggle over it. But surplus labour was transparent in modes of production previous to capitalism. In slave economies, the elite owned human labour who provided services without limit. In feudal economies, serfs worked specific hours or days and provided services for the lords. But in capitalist economies, it appeared that human labour power was exchanged for wages in a free and equal exchange.

But Marx showed that this was a sham. Surplus labour was still being extracted without payment because wages were paid for workers to meet their needs but they contracted to work for longer hours, days or years than the value contained in the purchasing power of their wages. Surplus labour took the form of surplus value in an economy where all the products of labour power were sold on a market as commodities, including labour power itself.

The classical economists had recognised that 'value' in the production of goods and services should be best measured in labour time. But they did not recognise that this was a disguised form of exploitation that created not just value, but surplus value. As Engels put it in his memorial address at Marx's funeral, *"Marx also discovered the special law of motion governing the present-day capitalist mode of production, and the bourgeois society that this mode of production has created. The discovery of surplus value suddenly threw light on the problem, in trying to solve which all previous investigations, of both bourgeois economists and socialist critics, had been groping in the dark."*

Marx too recognised the discovery of surplus value as his most important contribution. In a letter to Engels written at the time of the first volume of *Capital*, Marx described what he saw as the novelty of his work in relation to the political economy.

"The best things about my work are: 1) the fact that from the first chapter (on which all the intelligence of the facts relies) I show the double nature of labour, expressed on the one hand in the use value and on the other in the exchange value; and 2) it treats surplus value (Mehrwert) independently of its specific incarnations as profit, interest, land rents, etc."

Marx outlined his category of surplus value in Grundrisse notes in 1858. He noted that the category of surplus-value was missing in the work of the bourgeois economists and writes: *"... strictly speaking surplus-value-insofar as it is indeed the basis of profit but is still distinguished from the commonly so-called profit-has never been developed." The difference between profit and surplus-value does not exist for him (Ricardo)...profit is not understood as a self-derivative, secondary form of surplus-value".*

Engels explained Marx's discovery in his preface to Capital. *"The existence of that part of the value of products which we now call surplus-value had been ascertained long before Marx. It had also been stated with more or less precision what it consisted of, namely, of the product of the labour for which its appropriator had not given any equivalent. But one did not get any further. Some — the classical bourgeois economists — investigated at most the proportion in which the product of labour was divided between the labourer and the owner of the means of production. Others — the Socialists — found that this division was unjust and looked for utopian means of abolishing this injustice. They all remained prisoners of the economic categories, as they had come down to them."*

Now Marx appeared upon the scene. *"He analysed labour's value-producing property and was the first to ascertain what labour it was that produced value, and why and how it did so. ... By substituting labour-power, the value-producing property, for labour he solved with one stroke one of the difficulties which brought about the downfall of the Ricardian school, viz., the impossibility of harmonising the mutual exchange of capital and labour with the Ricardian law that value is determined by labour. ... He analysed surplus-value further and found its two forms, absolute and relative surplus-value. And he showed that they had played a different, and each time a decisive role, in the historical development of capitalist production. On the basis of this surplus-value he developed the first rational theory of wages we have, and for the first time drew up an outline of the history of capitalist accumulation and an exposition of its historical tendency."*

Marx's discovery of surplus value formed part of his theory or law of value based on living human labour. His other key laws of motion of capitalism were his law of accumulation and his law of the tendency of the rate of profit to fall. In Grundrisse, Marx worked out in detail the law of the tendency of the profit-rate to fall and characterized it as *"the most important law of modern political economy..., which despite its simplicity has never been understood up till now and even less has been consciously expressed"*. The consequence of this law is that *"beyond a certain point, the development of the productive forces is a barrier for capital; this means that the capital relation is a barrier for the development of the productive forces of labour."*

And thus *"The growing unsuitability of the productive development of society for its prevailing production relations is expressed in the slashing contradictions, crises and convulsions.... the highest development of productive power together with greatest expansion of existing wealth will coincide with depreciation of capital, degradation of the labourer, and a most straightened exhaustion of his vital powers." "... these regularly recurring catastrophes lead to their repetition on a higher scale, and finally to its (i.e., capital) violent overthrow."*

All three laws are integrally connected and in the next chapter they will be considered in order. The laws of value and accumulation appeared in Volume One of Capital. But the law of profitability did not appear until the publication of Volume Three in 1894. Grundrisse was not available to anybody until well into the 20th century.

This has led to much confusion on the validity of the law of profitability, its relationship with the other key laws and even on whether Marx eventually decided in the 1870s that the law was wrong and so dropped it, suggesting that Engels should never have included it in Volume Three, and by doing so, unnecessarily enhanced its importance.

The great Marxist revolutionaries who followed Marx's death in 1883 never really 'connected' with the law of profitability and to this day it is a minority of Marxist economists who consider the law as correct, logical, empirically valid and key to a theory of crises under capitalism. Rosa Luxemburg considered Volume Three as *"too scientific"* and the Bolshevik theorists like Lenin and Trotsky either ignored it or like Bukharin reduced its role to insignificance. Indeed, only a few Marxists during the 1930s, notably Henryk Grossmann, thought it central to Marx's economics. Later in the 1970s, most Marxists abandoned it or attempted to refute it, adopting Keynesian analysis instead. But more recently, several Marxist economists have revived Marx's law of profitability as central to the theory of crises under capitalism and the basis of the transient nature of the capitalist mode of production.

In my view, Marx never abandoned any of the laws that he developed in that 1850s period in London. In 1866 Marx decided to write four books on *Capital* which were to appear in three volumes: Volume 1 was planned to contain the first book on the "process of production" as well as the second book on the "process of circulation", volume 2 was to comprise the "structure of the process as a whole" and volume 3 the fourth book "on the history of the theory".[4] After having finished the first book Marx decided to publish this one as his first volume. He then wanted the second and third book to follow in volume two, and to close his work with the fourth book forming volume three.[5] It was not until Engels published the second book as volume two and the third book as volume three that today's view of *Capital* as being divided into three volumes was formed.[6]

As the latest scholarship on Marx's writings in the 1860s and 1870s reveals, Engel's edited version of Volume 3 is a faithful and accurate representation of Marx's original manuscript. In Volume Three, Marx's law of profitability was edited by Engels into three chapters. Some scholars now argue that Engels distorted Marx's view on the law of profitability from doubt to certainty. Be that as it may (and the debate on this continues), there is no evidence that Marx abandoned or disowned his law of profitability.

On the contrary, there is considerable evidence in Marx's correspondence, spanning the period from 1865 to 1877 that he was satisfied with his theoretical results and that he regarded Capital, not only the first volume that he published but also the volumes that remained unpublished, as a finished product in a theoretical sense. On July 31, 1865, he wrote to Frederick Engels that *"[t]here are 3 more chapters to be written to complete the theoretical part (the first 3 books). Then there is still the 4th book, the historical-literary one, to be written, which will, comparatively speaking, be the easiest part for me, since all the problems have been resolved in the first 3 books, so that this last one is more by way of repetition in historical form. But I cannot bring myself to send anything off until I have the whole thing in front of me. Whatever shortcomings they may have, the advantage of my writings is that they are an artistic whole, and this can only be achieved through my practice of never having things printed until I have them in front of me in their entirety."*[7]

This letter indicates that Marx had resolved, to his satisfaction, all of the theoretical problems he had confronted. He would not allow volume 1 of Capital to be published until the whole of Capital was complete in a theoretical sense. Thus, the publication of volume 1 a couple of years later is further evidence that Marx regarded the whole of Capital as complete and satisfactory in a theoretical sense. Indeed, in 1875, Marx wrote a 130-page manuscript that had to do mainly with the falling rate of profit and the relation between the rate of surplus-value and the rate of profit. Using many numerical examples and algebraic calculations, Marx traced the changes in the rate of profit of a particular capital over time, and also compared the rates of profit of two different capitals in different industries at the same time. He aimed to list all possible cases by simultaneously considering variations to both individual and multiple determining factors. Marx clearly planned to revise Volume Three just as he always tried to revise every planned publication to the bitter end. But the changes he envisaged in no way suggest a break with his law.

Other scholars have argued that Marx dropped the law as being useful in any way in the 1870s when he too found it illogical and irrelevant to crises. This seems a strange conclusion. Did Marx really change his view from a letter to Engels in 1868 that the law *"was one of the greatest triumphs over the asses bridge of all previous economics"*? And if he had dropped it, surely he would have informed Engels as he wrote his 130-page manuscript developing his profitability law in 1875.

After all, from 1870, Engels had moved from Manchester, so Marx and he met together as a matter of routine, usually daily. Discussions could go on into the small hours. Marx's house lay little more than 10 minutes walk away ... and there was always the Mother Redcap or the Grafton Arms.

Marx was a scholar who was seldom content with the work he had done, especially when it came to his work on economics. Already in 1858, he admitted that *"the final elaboration"* was progressing very slowly *"because subjects on which one has spent years and years of study and which one believes to have finally dealt with, consistently show new sides to themselves and raise new concerns."*[8]

He also mentioned that his *"peculiar method"* was characterized by the fact that *"if I return to some writings which I finished four weeks previously, I then find them inadequate and revise them again completely."*[9] In his sporadic remarks with regard to his project *Capital* in the 1870s and 1880s we find similar ideas. In the middle of 1871, for instance, Marx told Danielson that he had *"decided that a complete revision of the manuscript is necessary"*[10], ten years later he indicated plans to revise his entire work, including the first volume.[11]

Marx's thinking was always evolving, always open-minded and searching. Engels once stated: *"I had really begun to suspect from one or two phrases in your last letter that you had again reached an unexpected turning-point which might prolong everything indefinitely."*[12] Therefore, the analysis of former drafts and manuscripts that were not destined to be published by Marx himself appears to be worthwhile, in order to understand more clearly the development of Marx's thinking over the years.

Yes, Engels made significant editorial changes to Marx's writing on the law as in capital Volume 3. He divided it into three chapters 13-15; 13 was the law; 14 covered 'counteracting influences' and 15 described the internal contradictions. But in doing so, Engels shifted some of the text into Chapter 13 on the 'law as such' when in Marx's manuscript, the original came after the counteracting factors in Chapter 14. In this way, Engels actually made it appear that Marx balances the counter-tendencies in equal measure with the law as such, when the original order of the text re-emphasises the law after talking about counter influences. So, as Seigel puts it: *"Engels made Marx's confidence in the actual operation of the profit law seem weaker than Marx's manuscript indicates it to be."* [13]

Fred Moseley recently introduced a new translation into English of Marx's four drafts for Volume 3 of Capital by Regina Roth, where Marx's law of profitability is developed and showing how Engels edited those drafts for Capital[14]. Moseley shows that much maligned Engels did a solid job of interpreting Marx's drafts and there was no real distortion. *"One can, therefore, surmise that Engels' interventions were made on the basis that he wished to make Marx's statements appear sharper and thus more useful for contemporary political and societal debate, for instance, in the third chapter, on the tendency of the rate of profit to fall."*[15]

So let us now consider Marx's three laws of motion of capitalism.

CHAPTER 2
Marx and the three laws of motion under capitalism

The basis of Marx's economic analysis is his three laws of motion of capitalism. They are the law of value, the law of capitalist accumulation and the law of profitability (or more accurately, the law of the tendency of the rate of profit to fall). Starting with the law of value and connecting that to the law of capitalist accumulation and then onto the law of profitability, leads to Marx's theory of crises under capitalism and shows the ultimately transient nature of the capitalist mode of production in human social organisation.

Was Marx being precise when he used the term 'law' to identify his key analyses of capitalism? A hypothesis is a proposition or statement that can be tested. A theory goes further. A theory is a generalised set of principles to explain something and has been supported by observations and evidence. A scientific law is a precise mathematical relationship that is found to be true. Thus there is Newton's law of gravity or Einstein's $e=mc^2$, both of which can be precisely defined and are consistently true.

I would say that Marx's three laws meet this criterion. They are more than hypotheses to be tested; and they are more than just theories with predictive power and empirical backing; they are laws that have precise formulations and are consistently true. That's a strong claim.

The law of value
Marx's law of value starts with the obvious and self-evident reality that nothing of 'value' can be produced unless human beings exert energy to fashion something of new value to the producer or the consumer from something; humans using wool to spin it into textile, for example. If human labour is not employed, then nothing happens. As Marx put it:

"Every child knows, too, that the volume of products corresponding to the different needs require different and qualitatively determined amounts of the total labour of society. That this necessity of the distribution of social labour in definite proportions cannot possibly be done away with by a

particular form of social production but can only change the mode of its appearance, is self-evident .... Science consists precisely in demonstrating how the law of value asserts itself". [16]

In his great economic work, Capital, Marx did not start his analysis of capitalism with labour but with the nature of commodities i.e. the produce of labour sold on the market for money. Marx did that because he wanted to show that a commodity has a dual property: it can be used to satisfy needs and it can also be exchanged. So it contained both a use value and an exchange value. The value of every commodity (whether a physical thing or a service provided) has this dual character.

Marx showed that in exchange commodities are compared to each other. For example, when we say that a commodity contains value, then we recognise essentially that x quantity of commodity A is equal to y quantity of commodity B or z quantity of gold, and so forth. It follows that commodities must have something in common; otherwise, there is no basis for their comparison and exchange. The property that gives to commodities exchange value and thus makes them comparable must be distinguished from the measurement of their value.

That's where labour comes in. In fact, by experimenting with different properties of commodities, Marx ends up with the idea that the only economically meaningful property characterising all commodities is that they are all products of human labour. This common property allows the comparison of commodities according to the quantity of labour (measured in time) that they contain. Consequently, labour that is employed in the production of commodities gives them their value.

The dual nature of the commodity corresponds to the dual nature of labour. There is *concrete labour*, the different types of labour employed in producing different commodities; and *abstract labour*, where the labour is generalised to all commodities and measured in labour time. This abstraction allows the realisation of the exchange. It is the necessity of commodity producers to go on to the market and exchange their products that leads to the transformation of various 'concrete', useful labours into units of 'abstract' social labour. Under capitalism, all products of labour become commodities for sale at an exchange value. So the different types of (concrete) labour are 'abstracted' as the different products of labour are sold as commodities on the market at a price.

Money is the 'universal commodity' because it is the commodity (gold usually) accepted by all when exchanging commodities. *"Since all other commodities are merely particular equivalents for money, the latter being their universal equivalent, they relate to money as particular commodities relate to the universal commodity."* (Marx). So money becomes the expression of the 'abstract labour' in commodities.

The total 'abstract' labour time that goes into the production of commodities can be divided between direct labour time (the time taken by humans working) and the indirect labour time (incorporated in the non-labour inputs of machinery and raw materials). Or in other words, the value of any commodity is composed of living labour (humans) and dead labour (machines), measured in labour hours (as 'abstracted' by the market).

Under capitalism, human labour power itself is a commodity to be sold on the market. Indeed, this is a key characteristic of the capitalist mode of production where the majority have no means of production and so must sell their labour power to the owners of the means of production. So, just as with other commodities, labour has a dual property. On the one hand, it is useful labour, that is, expenditure of human labour in a concrete form and for a specific purpose and with this property creates use values. On the other hand, it is abstract labour, that is, expenditure of human 'labour power' without specific characteristics which creates the value of the commodity in which it is represented. Thus Marx made the distinction between labour and labour power, a distinction that is absolutely crucial for the understanding of the source of profit. *"By labour-power or capacity for labour is to be understood the aggregate of those mental and physical capabilities existing in a human being, which he exercises whenever he produces a use-value of any description."*[17]

Here is the great discovery in Marx's law of value. The labour time embodied in the commodities normally purchased by the worker for the reproduction of himself and his family in a day is less than the labour time that a worker actually offers to the owner of capital during the same time period. The result is that for any given time period, the worker produces more value than the wage equivalent which is paid by the owner of capital for the use of the labour power. This difference, Marx calls "unpaid labour" or "surplus labour"- or surplus value. Marx calls that part of total capital that pays wages, variable capital. The name is not accidental; it indicates that labour power enters in the process of production as the price of labour power (i.e., wage) and generates more value than the value required for of its own reproduction.[18]

Total value in labour time produced by Living Labour

The working day

Paid labour = value of labour power = wages	Unpaid labour = surplus value = profits, interest, rent

x labour force (3 bn) =
total hours of labour divided into value of
labour power and surplus value

Marx was the first to argue that in capitalism workers are exploited not because they are not paid their full wage, but because even when they are paid their full wage they can only buy the basket of goods required for the reproduction of their capacity to work (their labour power), which is acquired through what is only a portion of the total labour time that they expend during a workday. The difference between total labour time and that required to reproduce the workers' capacity to work i.e. surplus labour time and its monetary expression, the surplus value, is appropriated by the propertied classes (capitalists and landlords) and the state. The wealth accumulated in a society is directly related to the amount of surplus labour time, which is inversely related to the necessary labour time.

But there's more. The value of a commodity is only equal to the quantity of the abstract labour time that is 'socially necessary' for the production of the commodity in question. According to Marx, the labour-time socially necessary is that required to produce an article or service under normal conditions of production and with the average degree of skill and intensity prevalent at the time.[19]

There is also a dual character to being 'socially necessary'. A Rolls Royce car may have an expensive value in labour hours, machinery and technique, but if the whole of production was just devoted to making Rolls Royces, then there would be no food, houses, or general transport. So then a Rolls Royce would be valueless. Commodities have different degrees of social necessity. But social need for each commodity is not 'planned' by the conscious decisions of people, but by the social relations of the owners of the means of production and the labour force. Rolls Royces have only use value to the rich and only the rich can afford to buy them. As such, demand for goods and services will continually vary according to the balance of class forces and the 'effective' ability to pay for them. Demand is not autonomous from value creation and its distribution.

Market prices of commodities in the shops, on the internet and in trade are regulated by the average labour time socially necessary to produce them. Market prices go up and down and never cease to move, but the underlying anchor or regulator of those prices is the law of value, the average labour time involved: *"value plays the role of regulator, establishing equilibrium in the distribution of social labour among various branches of the national economy (accompanied by constant deviations and disturbances)."*[20]

The analysis of money leads to an investigation of the capitalist process of production. This process is described by the circuit M – C (LP, MP) ... P ... C0 – M0, according to which capitalists invest an amount of money (M) in order to buy a set of commodities (C) consisting of commodity labour power (LP) – that is, the worker's capacity to work – and other means of production (MP), for the purpose of production (P) of a new set of commodities (C0), which when sold they expect to realise a sum of money greater than that of the initial investment, M0 > M. This extra money is what really motivates the whole circuit of capitalist production as it is repeated on an expanded scale.

Hence, the value of a commodity is measured as the socially necessary labour time that is directly and indirectly incorporated in a commodity. This is the regulator of the movement of market prices. For Marx, the law of value is like Newton's law of gravity *"because, in the midst of all the accidental and ever fluctuating exchange-relations between the products, the labour-time socially necessary for their production forcibly asserts itself like an over-riding law of nature. The law of gravity thus asserts itself when a house falls about our ears. The determination of the magnitude of value by labour-time is therefore a secret, hidden under the apparent fluctuations in the relative values of commodities."[21]*

This is a law because it can be expressed mathematically and has been tested empirically in various studies. Cockshott and Cottrell[22] broke down the economy into a large number of sectors to show that the monetary value of the gross output of these sectors correlates closely with the labour concurrently expended to produce that gross output[23]. Anwar Shaikh also did something similar. He compared market prices, labour values and standard prices of production calculated from US input-output tables and found that on average labour values deviate from market prices by only 9.2 per cent and that prices of production (calculated at observed rates of profit) deviate from market prices by only 8.2 per cent.[24] Lefteris Tsoulfidis and Dimitris Paitaridis[25] investigated the question of price-value deviations using the input-output Table of Canada. They found for the Canadian economy the results are consistent with Marx's law of value. And G Carchedi, in a recent paper, showed that the validity of Marx's law of value can be tested with official US data, which are deflated money prices of use values. He found that money and value rates of profit moved in the same direction (tendentially downward) and tracked each other very closely.[26]

The law of accumulation
That brings us to what Marx calls the general law of capitalist accumulation. Capitalist production has a fundamental dynamic, the dynamic of accumulation, in which the scale of capitalist production constantly expands.[27] As Marx puts it in Capital: *"Accumulate, accumulate! That is Moses and the prophets! Industry furnishes the material which saving accumulates. Therefore, save, save, i.e., reconvert the greatest possible portion of surplus-value, or surplus-product into capital! Accumulation for accumulation's sake, production for production's sake: by*

this formula classical economy expressed the historical mission of the bourgeoisie."[28]

Marx is saying that competition among capitalists forces them to continue to expand their production in order to accumulate more profit or be driven out of business by others. So the law of capitalist accumulation says that competition makes each individual capitalist keep constantly extending capital[29]. The trend is for the proportion of the economy devoted to investment in the means of production (machinery, plant, offices, raw materials) to rise. This has happened pretty much from the point of Marx's birth in all capitalist economies.

The increasing scale of accumulation also produces qualitative changes.

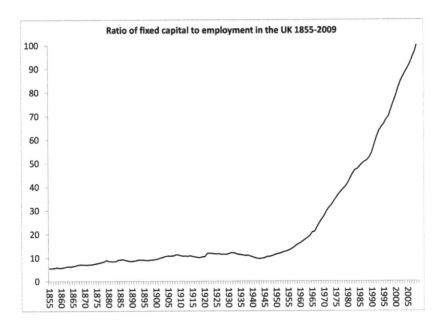

The rise of the stock of means of production under capitalism

Not all investment is the same. Investment in means of production, Marx calls 'constant capital' because means of production (a machine or raw material) cannot create new value on its own. So the value previously created to produce the machine is constant and cannot be increased. New value requires human beings going to work and turning on the machines and using up the raw materials. Only human labour power creates new value. To distinguish that, Marx calls the investment in human labour power, variable capital, because the value in that type of capital can vary (deliver new value).

The law of accumulation is that, as capitalists spend more of their profits on means of production, the ratio of the value of means of production compared to the value of the labour power employed would tend to rise. This ratio Marx called (rather oddly) the organic composition of capital. It is a law in capitalist economic expansion that the organic composition of capital will rise. As Marx says, *"The accumulation of capital, though originally appearing as its quantitative extension only, is effected, as we have seen, under a progressive qualitative change in its composition, under a constant increase of its constant, at the expense of its variable, constituent."*[30]

A relative diminution of the variable capital occurs in the course of the further progress of accumulation and of the concentration accompanying it. Ultimately, it is not the extensive growth of capital of the same kind, but the rising *"productivity of social labour"* that *"becomes the most powerful lever of accumulation"*[31]. This has meant living labour setting in motion a greater mass of dead labour. This in turn means a rising organic composition of capital as a greater value of constant capital is mobilised. The value composition of capital also tends to rise, but not as fast as the organic composition because, while the *"mass of means of production…increases…their value in comparison with their mass diminishes"* as rising productivity cheapens them.

This increase in the organic composition of the total social capital tends to reduce the relative demand for the labour power of workers by capitalists and can lead to increased unemployment as human labour is replaced by machines and technology. Thus there will appear an 'industrial reserve army', a layer of unemployed available to work but not being used. So the 'general law' of capitalist accumulation is that the capitalist mode of production tends to produce both increasing wealth in the hands of capitalists (machines, factories, cash etc) and increasing poverty suffered by workers (just wages and recurring unemployment).

Marx argues that the rising organic composition of capital means that a larger capital is required to maintain a given level of employment.

Thus accumulation must become progressively more rapid to maintain employment. At the same time, though, the rapid accumulation means a more rapid increase in the organic composition. Thus accumulation itself produces a *"relatively redundant working population"* (i.e. creates unemployment): this is the relative surplus population. *"[C]apitalist accumulation itself...constantly produces...a relatively redundant working population...which is superfluous to capital's average requirements for its own valorisation, and is therefore a surplus population* Although the *extensive accumulation can involve the drawing of new labour into production, as capitalism develops, attempts to raise the productivity of labour through increasing the organic composition tend to come to the fore. This means that alongside the "violent fluctuations" that temporarily create a "surplus population"—ie an economic downturn—there are longer-term tendencies leading to "the extrusion of workers already employed, or the less evident, but not less real, form of a greater difficulty in absorbing the additional working population through its customary outlets"* [32]

Because of the unevenness of capitalist development, this relative surplus population is constantly being created in some branches of production, and is often reabsorbed in others, and this is on an ever-increasing scale. This surplus population is a *"condition for the existence of the capitalist mode of production"* as the industrial reserve army that provides a mass of available labour power independent of the natural growth of population. The industrial reserve army also forces the employed workers to submit to intensified labour, so further reducing employment.

Marx considered the reserve army of labour to be an essential ingredient of capitalism, a relatively redundant population of labourers that would expand and contract according to the requirements of the system. As soon as the accumulation process diminishes this surplus population to the point of endangering the further production of adequate amounts of surplus value (by raising wages and other advantages of labour), a reaction sets in. The introduction of labour-saving machinery is quickened, the reserve army is replenished and the rise in wages is halted. Thus accumulation takes place as a cyclical oscillation: *"the general movement of wages is exclusively regulated by the expansion and contraction of the industrial reserve army and this corresponds to the periodic alternations of the industrial cycle"*[33]

Having created this surplus population, the latter becomes *"the lever of capitalist accumulation"*. As Marx writes: *"It forms a disposable industrial reserve army, which belongs to capital just as absolutely as if the latter had bred it at its own cost"*. This reserve army—the unemployed or underemployed—can be drawn into capitalist production when this expands or creates new fields of business. This is related to the economic cycle, which more generally causes fluctuations in the demand for labour. Indeed, the development of a reserve army allows capitalism to perform with greater ease its characteristic cycle of boom and bust. Along with technological change, another factor that increases the scale of the reserve army is the *"over-work of the employed part of the working class"*. The demand for increased labour power might be met simply by piling more work upon existing labourers, while condemning the unemployed to *"enforced idleness"*. There is no equitable distribution of labour among the population as a whole.

The development of a reserve army has implications for the wages of the working class. The pace and form of accumulation, and the corresponding division of the working class into employed and unemployed sections, result in the movement of wages. The growth of capital means a growth of wage labourers *"whose enslavement to capital is only concealed by the variety of individual capitalists to whom it sells itself"*[34]. So, since *"in each year more workers are employed than in the preceding year, sooner or later a point must be reached at which the requirements of accumulation begin to outgrow the customary supply of labour and a rise of wages therefore takes place"* As wages rise, two possibilities become apparent. Accumulation might be taking place on such a scale that it can tolerate the increase without it significantly impeding the accumulation. Alternatively, increased wages might start to slow the rate of accumulation, in which case the demand for labour-power will eventually slacken and the rise in wages decline or go into reverse. So the *"the rate of accumulation is the independent, not the dependent variable; the rate of wages is the dependent, not the independent variable"*.

The reserve army of labour is *"the background against which the law of demand and supply of labour does its work"*. The creation of this reserve army of labour is *"the absolute general law of capitalist accumulation"*. The paradox of this law is that developments such as the rise in productivity of labour, which ought in a rational world to benefit the labouring class as a whole, in fact *"distort the worker into a fragment of a man".. degrade him to the level of an appendage of a machine"* and *"alienate from him the intellectual potentialities of the labour process... Accumulation of wealth at one pole is, therefore, at the same time accumulation of misery...at the opposite pole".*

The drive to accumulate further entrenches capitalist relations. Accumulation tends to concentrate *"wealth in the hands of individual capitalists".* Along with the concentration of capital, there is also the "centralisation" of capital—the way that capitalist firms merge into bigger firms. *"The battle of competition is fought by the cheapening of commodities, which in turn rests on raising the productivity of labour. But the most successful capitalists in this area will tend to be the biggest, the ones who can mobilise every opportunity to invest in new machinery to render labour more productive. Therefore the larger capitals beat the smaller."* [35]

Over time (and after crises in production), this also involves both the increasing concentration of the means of production in the hands of ever larger capitalists, and the appearance of new capitalists in competition with one another. Apart from this concentration of capital that is a result of accumulation, there is also a centralisation of capital as more profitable capitals swallow up less profitable ones.

The law of accumulation is a law, first because it can be mathematically defined – C/V rises over time and despite any rise in labour productivity and falling value of commodities. And second, the law can be empirically verified and has been by many studies. Esteban Maito shows that the ratio between the volume of capital and production per person employed has risen across the world – a rising organic composition of capital. [36]

The law of the tendency of the rate of profit to fall

The first two laws of motion lead to the third law: the law of the tendency of the rate of profit to fall. The first law says that only labour creates value and the second says that capitalists will accumulate more capital over time and this will take the form of a faster rise in the value of the means of production over the value of labour power i.e. a rising organic composition of capital. So if the value of labour power falls relatively to the value of constant capital, then there will be a tendency for the increase in total value not to keep pace with the increased in invested capital (constant and variable). *"A fall in the rate of profit and accelerated*

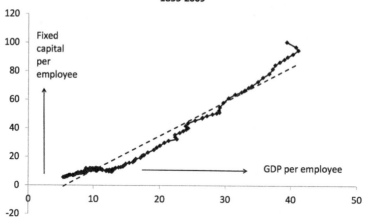

Productivity of labour and organic composition of capital in the UK 1855-2009

accumulation are different expressions of the same process only in so far as both reflect the development of productiveness. Accumulation, in turn, hastens the fall of the rate of profit, inasmuch as it implies concentration of labour on a large scale, and thus a higher composition of capital.[37] Thus accumulation is a process that inevitably leads to a surplus of capital unable to function profitably and an unusable surplus population.[38]

The bosses' appropriation of surplus value makes possible the expansion of capital, and it is made necessary by the class struggle of the producers against their exploiters. For Marx, the amount of surplus value extracted is the main issue in the class struggle between capitalists and workers. Capitalism expands by reinvesting the surplus value it appropriates: this is the basis of the accumulation of capital. As Marx put it, the *"aim [of the capitalist mode of production] is to preserve the value of the existing capital and promote its self-expansion to the highest limit (i.e., to promote an ever more rapid growth of this value. Capital strives to expand the value form even at the expense of developing use values."* The conflict of these tendencies, the most visible expression of the contradictions of value, is the key to the analysis of capitalist crises.

"The most important factor in this inquiry is the composition of capital and the changes it undergoes in the course of the process of accumulation". In the capitalist mode of production, and in that alone, is the development of the productive power not only expressed as a growth

of means of production in order to have more results with less labour, (as it is expressed in all economic systems) but as a rise in the organic composition of capital, more constant capital, less variable capital and a consequent falling rate of profit. This Marx called *"in every respect the most important law of modern political economy and the most essential for understanding the most difficult relations. It is the most important law from the historical standpoint. It is a law, which despite its simplicity, has never before been grasped and even less consciously articulated."*[39]

In short, technological innovations tend to decrease the average rate of profit because they tend to replace labourers with machines.[40] Since only labour creates value, the output per unit of capital may increase, but the value (socially necessary labour time) incorporated in that unit of output decreases. As Marx writes, *"The value of a commodity is determined by the total labour-time of past and living labour incorporated in it. The increase in labour productivity consists precisely in that the share of living labour is reduced while that of past labour is increased, but in such a way that the total quantity of labour incorporated in that commodity declines"*[41]. It follows that *"The rate of profit does not fall because labour becomes less productive, but because it becomes more productive."*.

Marx divides the total social capital into three broad categories: (1) constant capital (c), equivalent to expenditure on machinery, raw materials and heat, light and power. This capital was deemed constant in that it merely transfers the value embodied in it and cannot be the source of new value. (2) variable capital (v), the expenditure by capital on the purchase of labour power, variable because it is the only source for new value. (3) surplus value (s), the increment in new value accruing to the owners of capital. The rate of profit is given by surplus value over total capital: $s/(c + v)$.

Now as capital accumulates, there is a tendency for the constant capital to grow more rapidly than the variable portion of capital: this is the expression in value terms of the improvements in technology associated with capitalism throughout its history. The relatively rapid increase in constant capital as compared with the variable element of capital Marx refers to as the tendency for the organic composition of capital (c/v) to rise (the law of accumulation).

The simple formula for the rate of profit is s/(c+v); where s is the surplus value appropriated by the owners of the means of production from the total value created by labour; where c is the value of the means of production accumulated by the owners; and where v is the cost of employing the labour force to produce value. Marx's law *("as such")* of the tendency of the rate of profit to fall follows: if c/v rises, and the rate of exploitation, s/v, is unchanged, the rate of profit s/(c+v) must fall.

$$ROP = S/C+V$$

s/v/	ROP falls if C/V rises faster than S/V
c/v+1	C/V rises faster (tendency) BUT there are times when S/V rises faster (countertendency)

There are countertendencies to the tendency for the rate of profit to fall. That is why the law is a tendency. Marx lists several factors that could lead to a period of rising profitability. The two most important ones are when the organic composition of capital (c/v) rises but at a slower pace than the rise in the rate of exploitation (s/v); and when c/v falls because the value of the new means of production falls as a result of a greater productivity of labour incorporated into new technology.

Although an increase in the organic composition of capital will normally produce an increase in the rate of surplus value (s/v), or at least a rise in its mass (s), there are definite objective limits to such an increase, not least among them the actual physical limit to available working-time (nobody can work more than 24 hours a day, 365 days a year – and in fact way less physically). Also, there are social limits to working time – legal and moral. But unless s/v does rise with sufficient rapidity to compensate for the increasing organic composition (c/v), then the tendency for the rate of profit to fall will assert itself in an actual fall.[42]

Marx argues cogently that these counter-tendencies cannot predominate indefinitely or even for a long time, i.e. not more than several years or a decade or so – a small period in the history of capitalism. Eventually, in the long run, the organic composition of capital will rise more than the rate of exploitation rises and the rate of profit will resume its fall.[43]

A static system of capitalism is an impossibility; capital must either go forward, ie accumulate or collapse[44], as Marx argued in the law of accumulation. But accumulation presupposes profitable operation. But profitable operation depends on the lowering of the organic composition of capital and/or a rise in the rate of surplus value. This is where a crisis or slump in production comes in. The devaluation of capital as investment and production is stopped lowers the organic composition. In practice, this means the ruin of many individual capitalists. But from the point of view of total capital, from the point of view of the system, it creates the conditions for recovery.

The devaluation of capital is continuous anyway as it expresses increased productivity of labour. The price of computers is falling all the time. But in a crisis, devaluation of capital necessarily happens quickly and violently. So the crisis is a result of a fall in profitability and profits sufficient to cause weaker capitalists to go bust and stronger capitalist to stop investing and producing. Commodities cannot be sold, workers are laid off and cannot buy. Thus *the true barrier to capitalist production is capital itself*.[45] Overproduction of commodities is the result of overproduction of capital and this *is nothing more than overaccumulation of capital*.

Was Marx right about this law of profitability under capitalism? How did things pan out after Marx published Capital and after his death in 1883? Maito shows for Britain the connection between accumulation of capital, a rising organic composition, the reserve army of labour and profitability from 1855.[46] This seems to confirm Marx's analysis. Accumulation of capital rises faster than employment growth leading to a secular fall in the UK rate of profit. However, in certain periods, the inter-war period, accumulation of capital grew more slowly than employment and profitability rose. [47] For Marx, there is a unity in the law of value, the laws of accumulation and the law of the tendency of the rate of profit to fall.[48]

In my own work, from the analysis of the movement in the rate of profit from various sources, it is clear that there was a secular decline in the

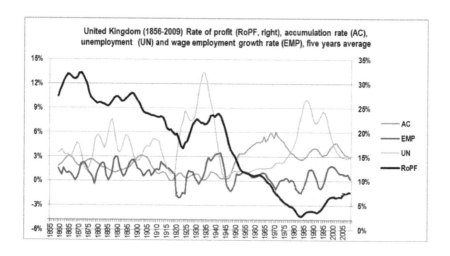

United Kingdom (1856-2009) Rate of profit (RoPF, right), accumulation rate (AC), unemployment (UN) and wage employment growth rate (EMP), five years average

UK rate of profit over the last 150 years, supporting the predictions of Marx's law and paralleling the decline of British imperialism.[49]

The periods of steepest decline in the rate of profit matched the most difficult times for British capitalism: the long depression of the 1880s; the collapse of British industry after 1918; the long profitability crisis after

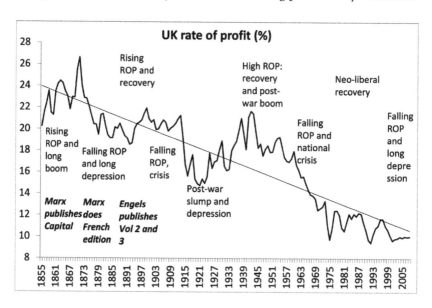

1946. But there were also periods when profitability rose: the recovery after the 1880s in the late Victorian era; the substantial recovery in the 1920s and 1930s after the defeat of the British labour movement and demolition of old industries during the Great Depression; and the neo-liberal revival based on further dismantling of the welfare state, the privatisation of state assets, the defeat of labour struggles and, most important, a switch to reliance on the financial sectors as Britain increasingly adopted rentier capitalism.

In the 1850s, British imperialism was at its height (after the 1851 Great Exhibition). It was the hegemonic capitalist power with dominance in industry, trade, finance, imperial incomes/colonies and armed forces. But by the end of the long boom up to the early 1870s, it began to give ground (relatively) to the rising economic powers of the US (now united after a civil war) and Germany (also now united) and to some extent France after the defeat of the Paris Commune in 1870.

During the Long Depression of the 1880s (and 1890s), Britain's hegemonic position was further undermined with the rise of Bismarckian Germany and America's growing industrialisation. And the period of economic recovery from the 1890s was weaker in the UK than in Germany or the US. UK profitability did not rise in the 1900s and, by the time of WW1, both Germany and the US could rival the UK's position.

The weakness of British industry and imperialism was exposed immediately after WW1. The UK rate of profit plummeted by 30-60% between 1914 and 1921. Britain entered a depression that was sharp and catastrophic to its ageing industry. The government tried to restore and preserve its hegemonic position globally in trade and finance by sticking to the gold standard. But this just weakened the position of British industry in global markets further, especially once France and Germany recovered from the war and Germany was relieved of the draconian reparations imposed under the Versailles treaty.

British capital then set about closing down old industries and reducing the share of value going to labour in a big way to restore profitability. This policy was cemented by the defeat of the transport unions in 1921 and the defeat of the general strike of 1926. The government came off the gold standard in 1925. This laid the basis for a sustained rise in UK profitability that even the Great Depression of the 1930s did not stop (in contrast to the US).

Profitability did fall during the worst years of the Great Depression 1930-32, but remained above the level of the early 1920s and recovered significantly from the mid-1930s. UK profitability was restored by the counteracting factor of an increased rate of exploitation of labour exceeding any rise in the organic composition of capital. In the 1920s, the rate of surplus value (exploitation) rose while the organic composition of capital fell (as old means of production were disposed of). In the 1930s, the impact of the Great Depression was to drive down the organic composition of capital even further, while the rate of surplus value stabilised.[50]

The profitability of capital reached a peak during WW2. This was partly the product of new profits from arms production, so that investment in productive 'civilian' assets fell, reducing the organic composition of capital. But it was also because the wages of labour were diverted into 'savings' (war bonds) that were utilised by the governments to pay for arms and the war machine. The rate of surplus value rose accordingly.

But after the war, British capitalism was in an exceedingly weak position, obviously compared to the US, but also compared to France and Germany (and even Japan), where American credit and capital was ploughed in to exploit millions of cheap labour and able to use the latest technology to boost productivity and lower unit costs to compete (with weaker currencies) on world markets. The UK had ageing capital stock and, while it had some new technologies to exploit, it had a small workforce unwilling to be exploited at low rates after being 'winners' in the war. So it was not long before UK profitability began to fall sharply.

All the major capitalist economies began to experience a 'classic profitability' crisis from about the mid-1960s. But the profitability crisis came earlier for the UK. As a result, it was also the first major capitalist economy to try and reverse the decline with policies of 'neo-liberalism' designed to raise profitability by increasing the rate of exploitation and privatisation of state assets that had been expanded in the immediate post-war period. Neoliberalism in the UK began as early as the end of the first simultaneous global recession of 1974-5, when the then Labour government called on IMF emergency funding and dispensed with so-called Keynesian government spending policies.

In summary, whenever the organic composition of capital rose faster than the rate of surplus value, the rate of profit fell, as in 1946-75. Whenever the reverse was true, the rate of profit rose, as in 1975-97. Overall, there was a secular fall from 1946 to 2008, when the organic composition of capital nearly doubled while the rate of surplus value rose much less. All this confirms Marx's law of profitability.

CHAPTER 3
Marx's theory of crises

Marx's theory of crises under capitalism flows from his three laws of motion in the capitalist mode of production: the law of value, the law of accumulation and the law of profitability.[51] Unlike these laws, Marx has a theory, not a law of crises. It's a theory because it is composed of various elements and levels of causation that must come together to produce a slump in production, investment and employment, which is the definition of a crisis.

Marx's theory of crises was not fully developed or explained by Marx during his lifetime. This has led to confusion and varying interpretations of the Marxist theory of crises and the debate over what Marx meant and more important, what is actually right continues today. In my view, Marx's theory of crises under capitalism has as its underlying basis, Marx's third law of motion of capitalism: the law of profitability.

As mentioned in Chapter 2, in Marx's view, the most important law of political economy was the tendency of the average rate of profit of capital to fall.[52] *In making this argument,* he posits the ultimate cause of capitalist crises in the capitalist production process, specifically in production for profit.

"The declining profit rate is in every respect the most important law of modern political economy, and the most essential for understanding the most difficult relations. It is the most important from the historical standpoint ... Beyond a certain point, the development of the powers of production become a barrier for capital; hence the capital relation a barrier for the development of the productive powers of labour. When it has reached this point, capital, i.e. wage labour, enters into the same relation towards the development of the social wealth and of the forces of production as the guild system, serfdom, slavery, and is necessarily stripped off as a fetter. The last form of servitude assumed by human activity, that of wage-labour on one side, capital on the other, is thereby cast off like a skin, and this casting-off itself is the result of the mode of production corresponding to capital; the material and mental conditions of the negation

of wage labour and of capital, themselves already the negation of earlier forms of unfree social production, are themselves results of its production process. The growing incompatibility between the productive development of society and its hitherto existing relations of production expresses itself in bitter contradictions, crises, spasms. The violent destruction of capital not by relations external to it, but rather as a condition of its self-preservation, is the most striking form in which advice is given it to be gone and to give room to a higher state of social production.[53] "

Tendencies and countertendencies

Marx's law is framed in terms of tendencies and countertendencies.[54] When new technologies are brought into the production process to increase efficiency, as a rule, assets replace labour and the organic composition rises. So the rate of profit falls. This is the tendency.

Why does Marx argue that the rate of profit tendentially moves downward? To increase their profitability, capitalists must increase their labourers' productivity. The way to do this is by introducing new means of production, which to increase productivity will usually shed labour. Capital-reducing investments could also be more productive. They would raise profitability but also free up capital for subsequent investment. After all capital-saving investments have been made, there will be *additional* potential labour-saving ones of which the most successful capitals can take advantage. So the general tendency is still for the organic composition of capital to rise.[55] Hypothetically, there might be capitalists investing in less efficient and thus lower-productivity means of production, which imply a lower organic composition of capital. But if they persisted in this choice, they would be doomed to bankruptcy. Thus, tendentially, due to the application of new technologies, the number of labourers per unit of capital invested falls, that is, the organic composition rises.[56]

There are also powerful countertendencies to Marx's law. Such countertendencies temporarily dampen or reverse the tendency of the rate of profit to fall. In particular, Marx mentions five countertendencies: (1) the increasing intensity of exploitation of labour, which could increase the rate of surplus value; (2) the relative cheapening of the elements of constant capital; (3) the deviation of the wage rate from the value of labour power; (4) the existence and increase of a relative surplus population; and (5) the cheapening of consumption and capital goods through imports.

In short, Marx's law of profitability goes as follows: as capitalism develops, the amount of constant capital rises in relation to variable capital. Because labour power hired with variable capital is the only part of capital that produces surplus value, the amount of surplus value falls relative to the capital invested. Capitalists consider the capital invested (especially labour power) as a cost. So this depresses the rate of profit unless there is a faster increase in the rate of surplus value, among other countertendencies. But the law will assert itself sooner or later as concrete reality.

These countertendencies introduce cyclical trends on the long-term trend of the downward rate of profit:[57] "*The operation of these counter-tendencies transforms the breakdown into a temporary crisis, so that the accumulation process is not something continuous but takes the form of periodic cycles.*" A crisis or slump in production is necessary to correct and reverse the fall in the rate and eventually the mass of profit.[58] In a period of depression and trough, some capitalists close down. Others can fill the vacant economic space. Production increases. Initially, net fixed investments do not rise. Instead, capitalists increase their assets' capacity utilization. So the means of production's efficiency does not rise, and the numerator in the organic composition of capital does not rise either. Also, due to higher capacity utilization, assets are subject to increased wear and tear, which reduces their value. Finally, the capitalists buy the means of production, raw materials, semi-finished products, of the bankrupt capitalists at deflated prices. Thus the numerator of the organic composition falls. Increased production with unchanged efficiency implies greater employment. So the denominator of the organic composition rises. The organic composition falls on both accounts, and the rate of profit rises. Rising employment increases labour's purchasing power and rising profitability increases that of capital. Both factors facilitate the realization of the greater output. So the upward profitability cycle generates *from within itself* the downward cycle. This latter, in its turn, generates from within itself the next upward profitability cycle.

The profit cycle – tendencies, triggers and tulips

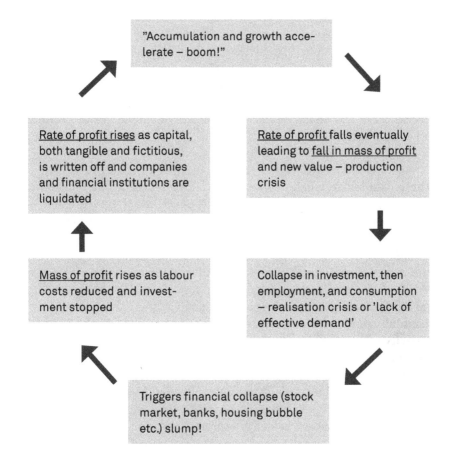

"Accumulation and growth accelerate – boom!"

Rate of profit rises as capital, both tangible and fictitious, is written off and companies and financial institutions are liquidated

Rate of profit falls eventually leading to fall in mass of profit and new value – production crisis

Mass of profit rises as labour costs reduced and investment stopped

Collapse in investment, then employment, and consumption – realisation crisis or 'lack of effective demand'

Triggers financial collapse (stock market, banks, housing bubble etc.) slump!

Crises and finance

While the underlying cause of crises is to be found in the general law of accumulation and the law of tendency of the rate of profit to fall (in what happens to capital in general in the production of surplus value), the actuality of crises can "*only be deduced from the real movement of capitalist production, competition and crises.*"[59]

Marx recognized that the possibility of breakdown in the circulation of capital was inherent in commodity production. The possibility of crises existed in the separation of sale and purchase in commodity circulation and in the role of money as means of payment. But this only raised the *possibility* of crises not their *regular cause*. That was the barrier set up by *"capitalist profit, which was the basis of modern overproduction."*[60]

That does not mean the financial sector (and particularly the size and movement of credit) does not play any role in capitalist crisis. On the contrary, Marx argues that the growth of credit and speculative investment in stocks, bonds and other forms of money assets (fictitious capital), appears to function as a compensating mechanism for the downward pressure on profitability in the accumulation of real capital.

A fall in the rate of profit inevitably promotes speculation; that is, trying to make money by betting on the stock exchange or buying other financial instruments. If capitalists cannot make enough profit producing commodities, they will try making money betting on the stock exchange or buying various other financial instruments. Capitalists experience the falling rate of profit almost simultaneously, so they start to buy these stocks and assets at the same time, driving prices up. When stock and other financial asset prices are rising everybody wants to buy them—this is the beginning of a 'bubble'. Such credit bubbles have been part and parcel of speculative investment, going back as far as the very beginning of capital markets - since the infamous Tulip crisis of 1637.[61]

If, for example, the speculation takes place in housing, this creates an option for workers to borrow (mortgages) and spend more than they earn (more than the capitalists have laid out as variable capital), and in this way the "realization problem" (sufficient money to buy all the goods produced) is solved. But sooner or later, such bubbles burst when investors find that the assets (mortgage bonds) are not worth what they are paying for them. Because fictitious capital is unproductive (ie it does not create any new value), fictitious profits are actually a deduction from real profits, which becomes clear when they are cashed in. Then the compensating mechanism of speculation fails and the result is even greater overproduction than was avoided before by the credit boom.[62]

Indeed, the "*so-called plethora of capital is always basically reducible to a plethora of that capital for which the fall in the profit rate is not out-weighed by its mass or to the plethora in which these capitals are available to the leaders of the great branches of production in the form of credit*".[63] Credit takes the accumulation of capital to its limit: "*if the credit system appears as the principal lever of overproduction and excessive speculation in commerce, this is simply because the reproduction process, which is elastic by nature, is now forced to its most extreme limit.*"[64] Thus "*a crisis must evidently break out if credit is suddenly withdrawn and only cash payment is accepted….at first glance the entire crisis presents itself as simply a credit and monetary crisis*".[65]

And each crisis of capitalism does have its own characteristics. The trigger in 2008 was the huge expansion of 'fictitious capital' that eventually collapsed when real value expansion could no longer sustain it, as the ratio of house prices to household income reached extremes. But such triggers are not causes. Behind them is a general cause of crisis: the law of the tendency of the rate of profit to fall.

In his lifetime, Marx witnessed two further crises after he had written Capital. In 1873 and 1882, he took the opportunity to explain the origins of this form of capital, be it public or private, in which "*all connections with the real process of valorization are lost until the last trace, and the representation of capital as an automat that expands its own value is consolidated.*" Fictitious capitals are "*accumulated claims upon production*". The question is whether such capital relates to a real accumulation process.

In analysing the crises of 1873 and 1882, Marx commented that loanable moneyed capital increases after a crisis, since there is more money seeking for investment opportunities that are no longer available. This is the main reason why crises are always preceded by a wave of optimism in financial markets, since there is a superabundance of loanable capital during prosperous periods, which causes a reduction in interest rates. Marx concluded: "*Altogether the movement of moneyed capital (as it expresses itself in interest) is the contrary of productive capital.*" Moreover, the crucial moment lies in the movement of productive capital.[66]

As Paul Mattick Snr has pointed out[67]:

"Although it first appears in the process of circulation, the real crisis cannot be understood as a problem of circulation or of realisation, but only as a disruption of the process of reproduction as a whole, which is constituted by production and circulation together. And, as the process of reproduction depends on the accumulation of capital, and therefore on the mass of surplus value that makes accumulation possible, it is within the sphere of production that the decisive factors (though not the only factors) of the passage from the possibility of crisis to an actual crisis are to be found ... The crisis characteristic of capital thus originates neither in production nor in circulation taken separately, but in the difficulties that arise from the tendency of the profit rate to fall inherent in accumulation and governed by the law of value."[68]

And, as G Carchedi put it after the Great Recession:

"The basic point is that financial crises are caused by the shrinking productive basis of the economy. A point is thus reached at which there has to be a sudden and massive deflation in the financial and speculative sectors. Even though it looks as if the crisis has been generated in these sectors, the ultimate cause resides in the productive (of surplus value) sphere, i.e. in the shrinking productive basis of the economy and in the attendant falling profit rate in this sphere, even though this downwards movement has manifested itself at first in the financial and speculative sectors".[69]

The problem is still the falling rate of profit, which depresses investment demand. If the underlying economy were healthy, an imploding bubble need not cause a crisis, or at least only a short one. If the total economy is healthy and the rate of profit is high, then the revenue generated will be reinvested in production in some way.

An artificial and temporary inflation of profits in unproductive sectors of a capitalist economy (like finance) can help sustain the capitalist economy and compensate for a falling rate of profit in productive sectors. But in a crisis, an increasing share of debtors who cannot finance their debt eventually causes default and the crisis erupts in the financial sector.[70]

Marx's law shows that the capitalist system does not just suffer from a 'technical malfunction' (Keynes) in its financial sector but has inherent contradictions in the production sector, namely, the barrier to growth caused by capital itself. What flows from this is that the capitalist system cannot be repaired to achieve sustained economic growth without booms and slumps—it must be replaced.

Both cyclical and secular

Is Marx's causal explanation of capitalist crises just that: a theory of recurrent and even regular crises, of booms and slumps in capitalist accumulation? Or is it more than that (or alternatively), a theory of breakdown, namely an explanation of how capitalism cannot continue indefinitely (even if it has regular crises), but must reach its limits as a system of social organisation, then break down and be replaced by a new system?

The answer is that Marx's theory of crisis is both cyclical and secular. His law of profitability suggests regular and recurring crises of over-production and slump followed by recovery for a while; but also an inexorable decline over decades (and longer) in the very profitability of capital accumulation, suggesting an end to capitalism.

As Maito concludes: "*The tendency of the rate of profit to fall and its empirical confirmation highlights the historically limited nature of capitalist production. If the rate of profit measures the vitality of the capitalist system, the logical conclusion is that it is getting closer to its endpoint. There are many ways that capital can attempt to overcome crises and regenerate constantly. Periodic crises are specific to the capitalist mode of production and allow, ultimately, a partial recovery of profitability. This is a characteristic aspect of capital and the cyclical nature of the capitalist economy. But the periodic nature of these crises has not stopped the downward trend of the rate of profit over the long term. So the arguments claiming that there is an inexhaustible capacity of capital to restore the rate of profit and its own vitality and which therefore considers the capitalist mode of production as a natural and a-historical phenomenon, are refuted by the empirical evidence.*"[71]

The law of profitability predicts that, as the organic composition of capital rises globally, the rate of profit will fall despite counteracting factors and despite successive crises (which temporarily help to restore profitability). This shows that capital as a mode of production and social relations is transient. Capitalism has not always been here and it has ultimate limits, namely capital itself. It has a 'use-by-date'.

Capitalism is not exhausted yet, however. The centre of capital accumulation has shifted in the last 200 years from Britain and Europe, in Marx's time, to the US and parts of Asia in the 20th century and now towards China and India. And there are still more areas to exploit labour power.

But Marx also looked for periodic crises to appear. His understanding of the recurrence of crises being integral to capitalism was already spelt out in the Communist Manifesto written in March 1848, just before the revolutions in Europe broke out. *"It is enough to mention the commercial crises that by their periodical return put the existence of the entire bourgeois society on its trial, each time more threateningly. In these crises, a great part, not only of the existing products, but also of the previously created productive forces, are periodically destroyed. In these crises, there breaks out an epidemic that, in all earlier epochs, would have seemed an absurdity — the epidemic of over-production.* "And how does the bourgeoisie get

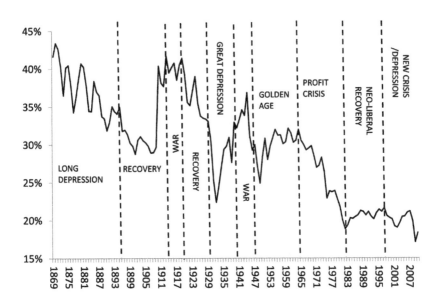

over these crises? On the one hand, by enforced destruction of a mass of productive forces; on the other, by the conquest of new markets, and by the more thorough exploitation of the old ones. That is to say, by paving the way for more extensive and more destructive crises, and by diminishing the means whereby crises are prevented."

But this was almost intuitive rather than based on a causal explanation of crises – still to come once Marx had developed his laws of motion. Once exiled to Britain after the defeat of the 1848 revolutions in Europe, he predicted a crisis for 1852. It actually started in 1854 and spread globally for the first time in 1857. Marx spent some time trying to calculate and measure the dimensions of that first international crisis of capitalism, just after he had formulated more clearly his theory of economic crises (as appears in Grundrisse and Volume 3 of Capital later).

Marx was continually searching for scientific explanations and evidence of this cyclical process. *"All of you know that, from reasons I have not now to explain, capitalistic production moves through certain periodical cycles".[72]* Marx commented that *"Once the cycle begins, it is regularly repeated. Effects, in their turn, become causes, and the varying accidents of the whole process, which always reproduces its own conditions, take on the form of periodicity"[73].* He wrote to Engels at the end of May 1873 about *`a problem which I have been wrestling with in private for a long time'.* He had been examining *`tables which give prices, discount rate, etc. etc.'. `I have tried several times -- for the analysis of crises -- to calculate these ups and downs as irregular curves, and thought (I still think that it is possible with enough tangible material) that I could determine the main laws of crises mathematically. [74]*

Marx saw the immobility of fixed capital as a part of the explanation of the periodicity of the cycle. He thought that the duration of the accumulation cycle (boom and slump) was about five to seven years, a view which he revised when the expected crisis did not strike in 1852 in favour of ten years. In the course of his research Marx developed the idea that the cycle was connected with the replacement of fixed capital. On this basis, he argued, *`there can be no doubt at all that the cycle through which industry has been passing in* plus ou moins *ten-year periods since the large-scale development of fixed capital, is linked with* *the total reproduction phase of capital determined in this way. We shall find other determining factors too, but this is one of them.'* [75]

Marx considered that *"So far the period of these cycles has been ten or twelve years, but there is no reason to consider this a constant figure."* Indeed, he thought that the cycle of replacement of capital would shorten. However, later Engels began to argue that *"the acute form of the periodic process, with its former ten-year cycle, appears to have given way to a more chronic, long drawn out, alternation between a relatively short and slight business improvement and a relatively long, indecisive depression -- taking place in the various industrial countries at different times."* [76]

Engels told Marx that it was normal to set aside 7 1/2% for depreciation, which implied a replacement cycle of 13 years, although he noted 20 and 30-year old machines still working. Marx concluded that *'The figure of 13 years corresponds closely enough to the theory, since it establishes a unit for one epoch of industrial reproduction which plus ou moins coincides with the period in which major crises recur; needless to say their course is also determined by factors of a quite different kind, depending on their period of reproduction. For me the important thing is to discover, in the immediate material postulates of big industry, one factor that determines cycles'.*

The key point for Marx was that *"the cycle of related turnovers, extending over a number of years, within which the capital is confined by its fixed component, is one of the material foundations for the periodic cycle [crisis] … But a crisis is always the starting point of a large volume of new investment. It is also, therefore, if we consider the society as a whole, more or less a new material basis for the next turnover cycle'.* So Marx connected his theory of crisis to cycles of turnover of capital. The accumulation of capital, including fixed assets, under capitalism depends on its profitability for the owners of capital. From that fundamental premise, if there is a replacement cycle of some duration in any capitalist economy, there is likely to be a cycle of profitability.

We can link the cycle of profitability to another cycle: the movement of share prices. The prices of the shares of US capitalist companies in aggregate also appear to move in cycles, with up and downwaves of about 16 years, very similar to the profit cycle. Investment analysts call the upwave in stock market prices, a bull market and the downwave, a bear market. These are very long periods for broadly one direction for stock prices to go. So these phases are called secular bull or bear markets.

The US stock market cycle follows a similar pattern to the profitability cycle. That close relationship can be established by measuring the market capitalisation of companies in an economy against the accumulated assets. Tobin's Q takes the 'market capitalisation' of the companies in the stock market (in this case the top 500 companies in what is called the S&P500 index) and divides that by the replacement value of tangible assets accumulated by those companies. On this measure, there was a bull market from 1948 to 1968, followed by a bear market until 1981 and then another bull market until 1999. The US stock market cycle appears pretty much the same as the US profit cycle, although slightly different in its turning points. Indeed, the stock market seems to peak in value a couple of years after the rate of profit does. This is really what we would expect, because the stock market is closely connected to the profitability of companies, much more than bank loans or bonds. When the rate of profit enters its downwave, the stock market soon follows, if with a short lag.

Can we talk about even longer cycles in capitalist production? Just as the capitalist profit cycle appears to be spread over approximately 32-36 years from trough to trough and so does the stock market cycle, there also appears to be a cycle in prices that is about double that size, or around 64-72 years. Such a cycle was first identified by Nicolai Kondratiev, a Russian leftist economist, in the 1920s. He argued that there appeared to be a period when prices and interest rates moved up for about a couple of decades or so and then a period when the opposite occurred.

Kondratiev followed Marx in reckoning these long duration cycles were based on the gestation period of large capital projects that could not be completed in the normal business cycle and so these investments would take place in a series of waves. He rejected criticism that any long cycles were caused by exogenous factors. *"Crossing through different stages, capitalism remains capitalism and maintains its basic features and regularities. Otherwise how could these stages be stages of capitalism?... I am not aware that the law of value and prices or the law of profit and its conjunctural fluctuations is absolutely different at different stages of capitalist development so as to preclude generalisation."*

There is also a cycle of economic growth and recession often called the 'business cycle' and first identified by the French economist Clement Juglar.[77] This now seems to be about 9-10 years, not dissimilar to the cycle that Marx and Engels discussed in the mid-19th century. This Juglar growth or business cycle has different turning points from the Marxist profit cycle, for two reasons. First, the cycle is of the whole economy, the productive and unproductive sectors, including the government sector. Thus the movements in the profit cycle and the productive sectors of capitalism feed through with a lag to the rest of the economy. Second, the Juglar cycle seems to be engendered by the decisions of capitalists to invest in constant and variable capital (machinery and workers). Profitability rises and, after a while, businesses start to employ more workers. As the cycle picks up, then they decide to invest more in machinery. This eventually leads to a fall in the rate of profit. Once this affects the *mass* of profit for capitalists across the board, they start laying off labour, making machinery idle or even closing down. And the stronger capitalists take over the weaker. This crisis takes some time to ensue after the profitability turning point. And the recovery also lags the recovery in profitability.

Finally, there is an even shorter business cycle of about 4-5 years. Joseph Kitchin discovered this in the 1930s. This cycle seems to be the product of even more short-term decisions by capitalists on how much stock to keep to sell. It seems that capitalists cannot see further ahead than about 2-4 years. They expand production and maximise the utilisation of existing production capacity. In the struggle to compete, capitalist producers end up with more stock than they can sell. So production is slowed until stocks are run down.

The profit cycle is key though. The upwave in the profit cycle from 1946-65 coincided with the upwave in the Kondratiev cycle. Thus the troughs in the Juglar cycles in the mid-1950s did not produce a very deep recession or downturn in economic growth and employment. High and rising profitability in an environment of a Kondratiev upwave was generally good news for capitalism: the golden age.

From 1965-82, the rate of profit fell. The Kondratiev cycle was still in an upwave of prices though. So what we got was successively worse

economic slumps (1970, 1974 and 1980-2) alongside rising prices —
in other words 'stagflation'. But in 1974, the Juglar and Kitchin cycles
troughed together and in an environment of falling profitability, world
capitalism suffered its first post-war simultaneous economic slump.
The 1980-2 recession was so deep and long-lasting because it was when
profitability reached lows and the Kondratiev prices cycle peaked.

The next upwave of profitability (1982-97) coincided with the downwave
in the Kondratiev prices cycle, which we are still in. Thus rising profitability was accompanied by falling inflation. Rising and high profitability
also meant that the Juglar growth troughs of 1991 and 2001 were not
nearly as deep or severe as 1974 and 1980-82.

After 1997, capitalist economies entered a profit cycle downwave, along
with the downwave in the Kondratiev cycle. With the collapse of the
credit fuelled boom in real estate in 2005-6, the Juglar cycle also fell and
this combination engendered the Great Recession and the subsequent
Long Depression, similar to the 1930s.

Alternative Marxist theories of crises
Looking for a cause is scientific. But dialectically there can be causes at
different levels, the ultimate (essence) and the proximate (appearance).
The ultimate is found from the real events and then provides an explanation for the proximate. The crisis of 2008-9, like other crises, has an
underlying cause based on the contradictions between accumulation
of capital and the tendency of the rate of profit to fall under capitalism.
That contradiction arises because the capitalist mode of production is
production for value not for use. Profit is the aim, not production or
consumption. Value is created only by the exertion of labour (by brain
and brawn). Profit comes from the unpaid value created by labour and
appropriated by private owners of the means of production.

The underlying contradiction between the accumulation of capital and
falling rate of profit (and then a falling mass of profit) is resolved by crisis,
which takes the form of collapse in value, both real value and fictitious.
Indeed, wherever the fictitious expansion of capital has developed most is
where the crisis begins e.g. tulips, stock markets, housing debt, corporate
debt, banking debt, public debt etc. The financial sector is often where the
crisis starts; but a problem in the production sector is the cause.

That is how I see Marx's theory of crisis. But some Marxists deny a role for Marx's law of profitability in his theory of crises. Instead they look to theories of disproportionality between accumulation and consumption (due to the anarchy of capitalist production); or the gap between the expansion of capitalist production and the 'limits of the market'; or to the lack of purchasing power for workers (a 'wage-led' crisis of 'realisation').

The disproportionality idea comes originally from the 19th century Russian economist, Tugan Baranovsky (who actually argued that there was no 'realisation problem') and Marxist Rosa Luxemburg (who did think there was one). According to Marx, crises can arise from disproportionalities within the production and circulation processes. Crises of this kind, arising exclusively from the disproportionalities of the system, are only an expression of the anarchy of capitalism and not of the exploitative character of the relations of production that underlie this anarchy; they are resolved, therefore, by the redistribution of surplus value, without the production of additional surplus value. The crises that arise from the nature of capitalist production, in contrast, do not solve themselves but can be counteracted only by the adjustment of surplus value production, that is, by an increase in exploitation.

It is not possible to separate the circulation process from the capitalist production process as a whole. This is precisely the fault of the two main distorted versions of the Marxian crisis theory, namely, the disproportionality thesis and the underconsumption thesis. What Marx shows is that if certain conditions of proportionality in the exchange between the two departments are observed no over-production of commodities would occur and reproduction on either a simple or extended scale could carry on undisturbed. That is to say, the general cause of the capitalist crisis cannot lie in the circulation process.

Marx recognized the problem of 'realization'. The anarchy within capitalist production and accumulation *permanently* excludes the realization of a part of the produced surplus value, so that the realized surplus value is always different from that produced. Whether commodities are over- or underproduced relative to the market can only be discovered after their production. The value and surplus value contained in unsaleable commodities is lost and cannot be capitalized. When the production oriented toward expansion reaches a point that puts its valorization in jeopardy, it ceases to expand and thereby produces an unsaleable mass of commodities whose value cannot be realized by accumulation and so cannot be realized at all.

In this way the suspension of accumulation appears as a problem of realization, since in fact produced commodities cannot be sold. Over-production, as the appearance in the market of the overaccumulation of capital, is only perceived in the form of the increasing difficulties of realization and is therefore explained in terms of them, although its real origin is the increasing divergence between production and value. Thus for Marx there are two sorts of realization problem: first, the ever present expression of capitalist anarchy; and second, the crisis problem, as the appearance on the market of the divergence between the profit produced and the surplus value requirements of an enlarged reproduction.

A more sophisticated version of disproportion theory was expounded by Bolshevik activist Pavel Maksakovsky.[78] Maksakovsky refers to Marx's law of profitability, but only to dismiss it as irrelevant to the cycles of boom and slump and, instead, focuses on Volume Two of Capital with its reproduction schema. He has a disproportion theory but with the addition of trying to show that the disproportion between the sectors of means of production gets *'periodically detached from consumption'*. But Grossman shows that Marx's schema do not show a *"widening and deepening contradiction"* between production and consumption under capitalism and so cannot be the Marxist expla-nation of recurrent crises. Investment growth is *always* outstripping consumption so cannot be the cause of *recurrent* crises.[79] To deny disproportion as the cause of capitalist crises is not to support Say's law (or 'fallacy', to be more exact) that 'supply creates its own demand'. The very process of exchange on the market creates the 'possibility of crisis'. But that does not explain the periodic and recurrent crises in capitalist production and investment.

In Marx, circulation and distribution are at a lower plane of causal abstraction, or if you like, closer to the proximate than the ultimate or underlying causes. A collapse in the stock market or in real estate prices will not lead to a collapse in production unless there are already serious difficulties in the latter. There have been many stock market collapses without a slump in production and employment, but not vice versa.

What the theorists of disproportionality crises forget is that Marx shows the necessity of crises, of over-production of capital, even *assuming* proportionality between departments of accumulation and consumption. While disturbances and disproportionalities are a continual feature of the capitalist system of production they are only partial in their effect, and since they are *always* present, they cannot be the explanation of the crisis cycle.

For Marx it is the discrepancy between material and value production that leads to difficulties in the accumulation process. The crisis is an overproduction of capital in relation to profitability or, what amounts to the same thing, an under-production of surplus-value in relation to the growing mass of total capital. *"An overproduction of capital, not of individual commodities, signifies therefore an over accumulation of capital-although the overproduction of capital always includes the over-production of commodities'...*

Carchedi comments: *"The disproportionality thesis submits that the root of crises lies in the difference between the technologically determined demand for specific use values as inputs of some branches and the technologically determined supply of the same use values as outputs of other branches. Marx's answer is that those " price fluctuations, which prevent large portions of the total capital from replacing themselves in their average proportions ... must always call forth general stoppages", due to " the general interrelations of the entire reproduction process as developed in particular by credit" . However, these are only "of a transient nature". Thus disproportions can either be determined by price fluctuations, and in this case they are self-correcting and cannot explain crises, or by lack of purchasing power, and in this case it is the latter, rather than disproportions, which explain crises. The disproportionality and underconsumption theories cannot account for the inevitability of crises; but, as we have seen, these theories do account for the inevitability of temporary and self-correcting disturbances. Only the approach linking insufficient production of (surplus) value with technological innovations can provide such an explanation."* [80]

The theory of 'overproduction' beyond 'the limits of the market' is really just the other side of the coin of underconsumption. Overproduction is when capitalists produce too much compared to the demand for things or services. Suddenly capitalists build up stocks of things they cannot sell, they have factories with too much capacity compared to demand and they have too many workers than they need. So they close down plant, slash the workforce and even just liquidate the whole business. That is a capitalist crisis.

Overproduction is the expression of a capitalist crisis. Before capitalism, crises were ones of underproduction (namely famine or scarcity). But to say overproduction is the *form* that a capitalist crisis takes is not to say it is the *cause* of the crisis. To say that crises are like a thunderstorm does not explain why we are wet. If it were the cause, then capitalism would be in permanent slump because workers can never buy back all the goods they produce. After all, the difference between what the workers get in wages and the price of the goods or services they produce that are sold by the capitalists are the profits. By definition, that value is not available to workers to spend, but is in the hands of the capitalist owners.

Marx criticised those capitalist economists who claimed that there could never be a crisis of overproduction because 'every sale that a capitalist makes means that there will be a purchaser'. As Marx said, that saying there is a purchaser for every seller is a tautology, as it is the very definition of exchange. Sure, *"no one can sell unless someone else purchases. But no one is forthwith bound to purchase just because he has sold"*. The money from a sale can be hoarded (saved) and not used to buy. That alone raises the possibility of overproduction and crisis. But the possibility of crisis in the process of capitalist exchange using money does not mean it will happen and provides no explanation of when or how. So Marx went further and explained that what will decide whether capitalists make purchases for investing in plant or new technology and to buy labour power to produce is the profitability of doing so. *"The rate of profit is the motive power of capitalist production. Things are produced only so long as they can be produced with a profit"*.

And this is where Marx's law of the tendency of the rate of profit to fall comes in. Marx shows that the profitability of capitalist production does not stay stable, but is subject to an inexorable downward pressure (or tendency). That eventually leads to capitalists overinvesting (over-accumulating) relative to the profits they get out of the workers. At a certain point, overaccumulation relative to profit (ie a falling rate of profit) *leads to the total* or *mass of profit* no longer rising. Then capitalists stop investing and producing and we have overproduction, or a capitalist crisis. So the falling rate of profit (and falling profits) causes overproduction, not vice versa.

As Henryk Grossman explained so well,[81] a falling rate of profit does not directly lead to a crisis as long as the mass of profit can rise. When a falling rate of profit eventually leads to a fall in the mass of profit and thus overaccumulation of investment and overproduction of goods and services (that are profitable), then the crisis ensues. It is precisely when the mass of profit stopped rising that the Great Recession ensued.

Thus the so-called realisation problem is the result of the production problem. Falling profitability and falling mass of profits lead to collapsing investment, wages and employment and then swathes of companies cannot sell their goods or services at existing prices and workers cannot buy them. This is a crisis of overproduction and underconsumption. Indeed, only Marx's law of profitability can explain the cycle of boom and slump, while overproduction or disproportion cannot do so.

Too much surplus, 'disproportion', 'overproduction' or 'underconsumption' are not Marx's theories of crises. But more important, they are very weak alternatives to Marx's law of profitability as an explanation. They are weak theoretically and even worse, empirically unverifiable. What are we measuring when we look at 'disproportionality' or 'underconsumption'? Does consumption fall before a slump? No, the evidence is clearly to the contrary, unlike profits and investment. Will disproportionate investment growth compared to consumption lead to overproduction and periodic crises? Well no, as Andrew Kliman has shown for the US.[82] Historically, business investment always grows faster than workers' consumption – that is the result of capitalist accumulation. But this does not create a chronic slump or permanent stagnation because investment creates its own demand (capitalist demand). Indeed, investment drives the productivity of labour and thus drives economic growth. The problem is when investment collapses, not when it grows 'too fast'.

Everybody in Marxist economic circles seemed to agree that the crises of the 1970s and early 1980s were the result of falling profitability rather than overproduction or underconsumption. But you see, the argument now goes, each crisis can have a different cause because capitalism metamorphoses into new forms or structures (neoliberalism or financialisation) that change the causal contradictions. And we are told that, because profitability rose after 2001 up to the Great Recession (actually only to 2006), Marx's law does not apply and we need to consider that the Great Recession was the result of either financial instability, excessive credit, rising inequality and falling wage share, or weak demand and secular stagnation.

Many Marxists reckon that to promote Marx's law of profitability as the underlying or ultimate cause of crises in capitalism is too 'reductionist' or 'monocausal'.[83] There are more dimensions or causes for crises. Well, the law may not be <u>sufficient</u> to explain crises, but it is <u>necessary</u>. Marx's approach was to abstract from reality the underlying essential (necessary) laws of capitalist motion and then add back concrete features of capitalism to reach the immediate. In that sense, Marx's law can be seen as the underlying or 'ultimate' cause of recurrent crises, which can be triggered by 'proximate' events i.e. (an oil price crisis, stock market bubble, or real estate crash etc). Then we have 'sufficient' causes.

Marx reminded his readers of this when discussing the 1857 panic: *"What are the social circumstances reproducing, almost regularly, these seasons of general self-delusion, of over-speculation and fictitious credit? If they were once traced out, we should arrive at a very plain alternative. Either they may be controlled by society, or they are inherent in the present system of production. In the first case, society may avert crises; in the second, so long as the system lasts, they must be borne with, like the natural changes of the seasons".*[84]

As Marx puts it, 'over-speculation and fictitious credit' arise from regular crises in the capitalist system of production. They cannot be eradicated by social action unless the mode of production is replaced. It is not possible to separate crises in the financial sector from what is happening in the production sector. *"That is to say, crises are possible without credit".*[85]

None of the alternatives to Marx's law as the underlying cause of crises seems convincing. As Alan Freeman recently said Marx's law of profitability remains *"the only credible competitor left in the contest to explain what is going wrong with capitalism".*[86]

CHAPTER 4
Marx's critics

The modern critics

Not long after the end of the Great Recession and with many economies still suffering from its impact, more mainstream economists started to refer to Marx for an explanation of what happened to capitalism before, during and after the Great Recession. Most of the new references have been accompanied by criticisms that generally dismiss Marx's theories and laws as being irrelevant and/or wrong.

However, George Magnus, senior economic advisor to UBS, the large Swiss investment bank, appeared favourably inclined to what he considers is a Marxist explanation of capitalist crisis. According to Magnus[87], Marx shows how, under capitalism, economic growth comes into conflict with the needs of private property. Magnus says that *"traditional economic analysis leads to traditional economic policy prescriptions, which are useless and inappropriate"*. The reason for Marx's relevance today is precisely because *"we are in a once-in-a-generation crisis of capitalism, triggered by the financial bust ... Marx analysed and explained insightfully how and why capitalism would succumb to recurrent crises, and especially big ones after a credit bust."*

Magnus goes on: *"The wily philosopher's analysis of capitalism had a lot of flaws, but today's global economy bears some uncanny resemblances to the conditions he foresaw. Consider, for example, Marx's prediction of how the inherent conflict between capital and labour would manifest itself. As he wrote in Capital, companies' pursuit of profits and productivity would naturally lead them to need fewer and fewer workers, creating an "industrial reserve army" of the poor and unemployed: 'Accumulation of wealth at one pole is, therefore, at the same time accumulation of misery'."*

According to Magnus, Marx also pointed out the paradox of over-production and under-consumption: the more people are relegated to poverty, the less they will be able to consume all the goods and services companies produce. When one company cuts costs to boost earnings, it's smart, but when they all do, they undermine the income formation

69

and effective demand on which they rely for revenues and profits. This problem, too, is evident in today's developed world. We have a substantial capacity to produce, but in the middle- and lower-income cohorts, we find widespread financial insecurity and low consumption rates. As Marx put it in Capital: *"The ultimate reason for all real crises always remains the poverty and restricted consumption of the masses."*[88]

Yet again, like other mainstream economists, Magnus sees Marx's theory of crisis as one due to extreme inequality of income and the weak purchasing power of workers. The issue of profitability is absent from his interpretation of Marx. Magnus' policy solutions, of course, fall well short of what Marx would have said. Magnus does not call for the replacement of this production for private profit system with one based on democratic planning for social needs. Of course not, instead he looks, as he says, to follow Keynes in order to find *"how capitalism could sidestep Marx's crises and controversial endgame."*

Magnus reckons we need to replace the delusions of mainstream economics with 'political economy' i.e. economics based on being aware of the social forces behind the economy (presumably meaning classes and vested interests). In addressing *"a very Marxist crisis of capitalism"*, he wants economic policy targeting job creation, income formation and economic growth. He comes up with the usual ragbag of Keynesian prescriptions, ranging from debt forgiveness for mortgage holders, tax cuts for business and inflation targeting driven by central banks printing money.

We get much the same policies being proposed by that longstanding Keynesian economist and writer for the *Financial Times*, Sam Brittan[89]. Brittan dismisses the idea that the current crisis is *'very Marxist'*, although he makes no attempt to explain the causes of the Great Recession himself. He quickly dismisses Marx's theory of value as *"too scholastic by half"* before telling his readers that Marx's *'ethical case'* against capitalism is also wrong. The case against capitalism for Brittan (assuming he is against it) is not *"the existence of a return on capital"* (i.e. the existence of profit) but that *"capital ownership is so highly concentrated"*. Brittan seems to be implying that if capitalist companies were small businesses, it would not be 'immoral' and there would be no reason to reject the private profit system. Well, capitalism is not structured like that now (if it ever was) and there is no possibility that large corporations can be broken up into small units that can 'compete'. This is the height of utopianism, something Brittan accuses Marx of.

Brittan attempts to explain Marx's crisis theory. Basically, *"the system produces an ever expanding flow of goods and services which an impoverished proletarianised population could not afford to buy"*. Thus he delivers yet again the underconsumptionist view of Marx's crisis theory. That and 'excessive inequality' seems to be the interpretation of Marx that all these mainstream economic gurus want to make. This is no coincidence. If you reckon that the lack of workers' purchasing power is the cause of crisis, then you can pose an easy reform solution for capitalism, namely more spending by government or the printing of money by central banks. Indeed, why not just bump up everybody's wages?

This is another indication that not only is the underconsumption explanation of capitalist crisis wrong, its reformist remedy is equally ineffective in 'saving' capitalism. For example, Brittan proposes mainstream stimulus measures as a way out. *"If the only thing that is wrong with capitalism is insufficient mass purchasing power, then surely the remedy is the helicopter drop of money envisaged by Milton Friedman"*. So we do not need a *"political revolution"* as Marx advocated, but just an *'intellectual one'* of ideas to persuade economists to support policies of stimulus rather than what Brittan calls *"a balanced budget fetish"* of austerity. But the lack of workers' consumer power is not *'the only thing wrong'* with capitalism. The unresolvable contradiction for capitalism lies in its inability to meet social need because of the limits of capital to reproduce itself and expand indefinitely, in other words, its inability to create enough profit.

Yet another mainstream economist has ventured to comment on Marxist economics. Bradford DeLong is a leading Keynesian economist.[90] DeLong notes that Marx refutes Say's law that supply creates its own demand and thus capital can reproduce itself in a balanced and equilibrium manner. De Long is upset that Marx does not credit John Stuart Mill with this observation (although Marx came to this conclusion about the possibility of crisis in the monetary means of exchange well before JS Mill). DeLong then notes that Marx reckons that crises come about because consumption falls as a share of output while investment keeps on rising. So here we go again with an under-consumption interpretation.

A few years ago the New York Times (NYT) launched a debate about whether Karl Marx was right after all about capitalism[91]. As the *NYT* put it in its introduction to the contributions of some well-known economic commentators and bloggers:*"in the golden, post-war years of Western economic growth, the comfortable living standard of the working class and the economy's overall stability made the best case for the value of capitalism and the fraudulence of Marx's critical view of it. But in more recent years many of the forces that Marx said would lead to capitalism's demise – the concentration and globalization of wealth, the permanence of unemployment, the lowering of wages – have become real, and troubling, once again. So is his view of our economic future being validated?"*

You could see what's was worrying the NYT. Like many supporters of capitalism as the only and best system of human social organisation, the NYT was worried that capitalism does not (or no longer seems) to deliver ever-increasing living standards for the majority, but instead is producing ever greater inequalities of wealth and incomes, to such a point that it could provoke a backlash against the system itself.

So the NYT offered a debate. And the question of whether Marx was right about capitalism was put to five bloggers. Free marketeer, Michael Strain, from the neo-liberal American Enterprise Institute, responded that maybe Marx had a point back in the days of Victorian England and Charles Dickens, when there was poverty everywhere. But now, things are different. Now only just over 5% of the world's population is living on less than $1 dollar a day compared to over 26% just 40 years ago. This is the great achievement of 'free enterprise'.

This statistic hides a story though, because the big reduction in the worst level of poverty living on $1 (1987 prices) was achieved by China's dramatic rise in the world economy and Strain would not conclude that China's economy is an example of 'free enterprise'. For that matter, the biggest falls in poverty in the 20th century also took place in the Soviet economies until the fall of the Wall.

No matter, after damning Marx with faint praise, Strain brings up a hoary old chestnut used by mainstream economics: the fallacies of Marx's labour theory of value. You see, it's obviously false *"that the value of an object is determined by the labour required to produce it. I could spend hundreds of hours writing a song; Bruce Springsteen could write one in 15 minutes worth far more than mine. Q.E.D".*

Well, fancy Marx not noticing that the product of some people's labour is worth more in the market than others even though they take less time. Clearly, Strain has not read Marx's Capital Volume One, where he deals with this issue and many others in relating the difference between 'concrete' labour and 'abstract' labour time- see my chapter 2.

But again, no matter, Strain had to admit that Marx may still have a point about capitalist crises: *"There is an inherent instability in capitalism — cycles of boom and bust lead to human misery. Capitalism does create income and wealth inequality."* That doesn't sound good for 'free enterprise' but Strain then told NYT readers that, after all, such crises are <u>not</u> 'inherent' and all this inequality and boom and bust were just leftovers from the Great Recession and capitalism would soon be all right. Strain's arguments are thin indeed.

And there's more again from top Keynesian Brad DeLong, professor of economics at University of California, Berkeley. First, he tries a quick demolition of *"Marx's fixation on the labour theory of value"* which according to DeLong *"made his technical economic analyses of little worth".* You see, Marx's claim that only labour creates value meant that he could not see rising living standards being achieved if the rate of exploitation of labour rose over time. Marx was *"confused between levels and shares"* of income. After all, you can have a falling share of value going to labour, but still have rising living standards.

This, of course, is yet another old chestnut: that Marx reckoned wages would keep on falling under capitalism until the point that, as DeLong puts it, the working class would starve. And how wrong was that. This is a nonsense view of Marx's 'immiseration' theory[92]. Marx clearly recognised that rising productivity of labour under the dynamic development of the capitalist mode of production could lead to increased wages, except that the workers would have to fight for them. A rising rate of exploitation did not necessarily mean falling wages, although sometimes it could. Again this is all in Marx's Capital – but our esteemed economist seems ignorant of that.

All these misrepresentations of Marx's value theory are deliberate. Marx's theory explains that the world's wealth does not come from capitalists investing, landlords from owning land or bankers from lending money, or somehow from 'technology', but from the effort of human labour. But the product of labour is usurped and appropriated by the owners of capital so there is a direct contradiction between profit and the value created by labour. This is something that cannot be admitted or accepted by the apologists of capital.

DeLong tells us that Marx thought that new technology under capitalism would lead inexorably to rising unemployment and Marx was wrong. But what Marx explained was that capital's drive for higher profits would mean more labour-saving technology. That would mean a rise in the ratio of machinery, plant and technology per employee, what Marx called the organic composition of capital. The evidence for this happening over time in every major capitalist economy is overwhelming. The ratio of the means of production to the employment of labour has risen hugely. And this creates a tension between capital and labour on sharing out the new value created and on the continued employment of labour in outdated industries. A reserve army of labour is permanently available for capital to exploit or not (the law of accumulation). This seems to describe exactly the nature of technology and labour under capitalism, not DeLong's distortion.

Tyler Cowan is a professor of economics at George Mason University. He is a firm proponent of modern neoclassical economics that starts from the assumption of free markets and sees economics as the study of the allocation of scarce resources, basing himself on the neoclassical assumptions of marginalism. For Cowan, Marx has got the wrong end of the stick. Capitalism's failure to provide things like decent education and health or better living standards, at least right now, is because of 'vested interests' blocking the free market from making a proper alloca-tion of resources. 'Rent seekers' and monopolies (including trade union interference) are the problem, not capitalism as such. Cowan reckons Marx has little to say on these issues. Again, of course, yet another eminent economist has not read his Marx, who dealt with the issue of monopoly and rent at length.

Like DeLong, Cowan confuses productivity with profitability. For him, the low profitability that Marx pointed out *"perceptively"* is due to the low growth in productivity since the 1970s. Thus Cowan suggests that Marx had a similar theory to the neoclassical marginal productivity theory, something by the way that Thomas Piketty also thinks in his recent opus, Capital in the 21st century. But turning Marx into a neoclassical economist won't work. Actually Marx's theory is the opposite: a higher growth in the productivity of labour will eventually lead to a falling rate of profit, because it can only be achieved by increasing investment in the means of production and reducing relatively the costs of labour. But as profits only come from labour power, there is a tendency for profitability to fall as productivity *rises*.

Yves Smith is the head of Aurora Advisors, a management consulting firm and generally considered more to the left in the economic spectrum. But she soon dismisses Marx's analysis, as she sees it, in her contribution. We are told that Marx had an underconsumption theory of crises under capitalism, namely that *"Marx believed that overproduction would lead to pressure on wages, which would prove to be ultimately self-defeating, since the drive to lower pay levels to restore and increase profit levels would wreck markets for goods and services. That's very much in keeping with the dynamic in advanced economies today."* This is the usual view of Marx by many lefts and the modern version of this is to claim that rising inequality of incomes is the cause of crises, or at least the latest one.

According to Smith, Marx got it wrong about class struggle under capitalism eventually leading to its overthrow. You see, a 'middle class' developed around managers and trade unionists and this has permanently blocked any move to end capitalism. So Marx was wrong in his expectation of change.

There was only one person who defended Marx's ideas out of the five invited to contribute to the NYT debate. Doug Henwood is editor of Left Business Observer, host of a weekly radio show originating on KPFA, Berkeley, and is author of several books. Henwood makes it clear where he stands: *"I don't see how you can understand our current unhappy economic state without some sort of Marx-inspired analysis."* Even better, he places the Marxist theory of the cause of crises under capitalism squarely with the movement of profitability. *"Corporate profitability — which, as every Marxist schoolchild knows, is the motor of the system — had fallen sharply off its mid-1960s highs."*

As Henwood explains, the strategists of capital moved to raise profitability through a reduction in labour rights and by holding down wages. *"The "cure" worked for about 30 years. Corporate profits skyrocketed and financial markets thrived. The underlying mechanism, as Marx would explain it, is simple: workers produce more in value than they are paid, and the difference is the root of profit. If worker productivity rises while pay remains stagnant or declines, profits increase. This is precisely what has happened over the last 30 years. According to the Bureau of Labour Statistics, productivity rose 93 percent between 1980 and 2013, while pay rose 38 percent (all inflation-adjusted)".*

However, Henwood reckons the <u>current</u> crisis is the result of inequality and low wages reducing consumption and thus the answer is to raise wages and public spending. The problem with this view is that it does not match the facts: consumption did not slump at all prior to the Great Recession: it was the collapse of the housing market, profits and then investment, not consumption. Raising wages and reducing inequality will help the majority but lower profitability further and thus reignite the capitalist crisis. It's not higher shares for labour that is the answer but the replacement of the capitalist mode of production.

But at least Henwood understands better Marx's views, unlike the others. That did not stop Philip Pilkington, a heterodox economist, telling Henwood that he was wrong. Pilkington correctly refuted DeLong's distortion that Marx thought wages must keep falling. As he says *"I don't know why this myth continues to bounce around. Everyone and their mother seem to think that Marx was dead sure that real living standards of workers could not rise under capitalism. But this is simply not true… Marx did not argue that real wages could not rise under capitalism. End of story."*

Unfortunately, Pilkington relies on the arguments of the post-Keynesian 'Marxist' economist of the 1940s, Joan Robinson. As a result, he claims that Henwood is *'confused'* to argue that US profitability fell in the 1970s. He says *"I don't know where this stuff comes from. I know that Marxists want to bring every crisis down to some sort of crisis of profitability but really, the data are readily available."* Yes, they are readily available and, unfortunately for Pilkington, they back the Marxist case. Pilkington is *confused* with his data. Not understanding Marx's law of the tendency of the rate of profit to fall, Pilkington provides us with a graph showing the year on year change in the mass of profit to refute Henwood, not the rate of profit. Pilkington concludes with a question *"is Marx relevant for understanding the world today?"* And his answer: *"Frankly, I don't think so."* For him, we are back to rising inequality and banking speculation as the explanations of crises – they remain the most popular and yet the furthest away from Marx's.

More recently, Jonathan Portes, a leading mainstream Keynesian economist wrote a short book on capitalism[93]. Portes starts with defining a capitalist. *"Are you a capitalist? The first question to ask is: do you own shares? Even if you don't own any directly (about half of Americans do but the proportion is far lower in most other countries) you may have a pension that is at least partly invested in the stock market; or you'll have savings in a bank. So you have some financial wealth: that is, you own capital. Equally, you are probably also a worker, or are dependent directly or indirectly on a worker's salary; and you're a consumer. Unless you live in an autonomous, self-sufficient commune – very unusual – you are likely to be a full participant in the capitalist system."*

But for Marx, you are not a capitalist if you do not get your income predominantly from surplus-value (profit or dividends, interest and rent). And only a very tiny percentage of people of working age do. Indeed, Marxist economist Simon Mohun has shown that less than 2% of income earners in the US fit that bill.[94] Nearly 99% of us have to work (sell our labour power) for a living. Even if some of us get some dividends, or rent, or interest from savings, we cannot live off that alone. Yes, we workers 'interact' in the capitalist system but only through the exploitation of our value-creating (for capital) labour power. We are not a 'full participant' in capitalism, except in that sense.

Portes tells us that capitalism is constrained by laws and the state on our behalf: *"property rights are rarely unconstrained.... This web of rules and constraints, which both defines and restricts property rights, is cha-racteristic of a complex economy and society."* However, the idea that the state just arbitrates between capitalists and between capitalists and workers to ensure a 'level playing field' is an illusion. The state needs to control outright conflict between classes and individuals (over property rights), but its primary role is to deliver the needs of the ruling elite (*"the executive committee of the ruling class"* – Marx). In the case of capitalism, that means the interests of capital and the owners of the means of production.

But what did Marx get right, according to Portes? *"Marx had two fundamental insights. The first was the importance of economic forces in shaping human society. For Marx, it was the "mode of production" – how labour and capital were combined, and under what rules – that explained more or less everything about society, from politics to culture. So, as modes of production change, so too, does society."* Yes, social relations are determined by the mode of production – although, for Marx, labour and 'capital' only exist as real social categories in the capitalist mode of production. 'Capital' is not just the physical means of production or fixed assets, as Portes implies and as mainstream economics thinks. For Marx, it is a specific social relation that reveals the form and content of exploitation of labour under capitalism.

Portes goes on: *"The second insight was the dynamic nature of capitalism in its own right. Marx understood that capitalism could not be static: given the pursuit of profit in a competitive economy, there would be constant pressure to increase the capital stock and improve productivity. This in turn would lead to labour-saving, or capital-intensive, technological change."* Yes, Marx saw capitalism as a dynamic mode of production that would drive up the productivity of labour through a rise in the organic composition of capital, as never seen. But Portes significantly leaves out the other side of the coin of capitalism, namely that, while competition may drive capitalists to invest and boost the productivity of labour, there is a contradiction between the 'dynamism' of capitalism and private profit. A rising organic composition of capital tends to lead to a fall in the profitability of capital. Capitalism is not a permanently 'progressive mode of production', as Portes implies, but is flawed and ultimately fails at the door of sustaining profitability.

Portes says that Marx's critique of capitalism is based on the idea that the wages of labour would be driven to subsistence levels and this is where he was wrong. *"Though Marx was correct that competition would lead the owners of capital to invest in productivity-enhancing and labour-saving machinery, he was wrong that this would lead to wages being driven down to subsistence level, as had largely been the case under feudalism. Classical economics, which argued that new, higher-productivity jobs would emerge, and that workers would see their wages rise more or less in line with productivity, got this one right."* Portes claims that *"so far, it seems that increased productivity, increased wages and increased consumption go hand in hand, not only in individual countries but worldwide."*

Actually, Marx never had a subsistence theory of wages. On the contrary, he criticised fiercely such a view, as expressed by reactionary 'classical' economist Thomas Malthus and socialist Ferdinand Lassalle. Unfortunately, Portes accepts this common distortion of Marx's view on the relation between wages and profits. What Marx said was that wages cannot eat up all productivity, because profits must be made for capital. But the degree of the distribution between profits and wages is not fixed by some 'iron law' but is determined by the class struggle between workers and capitalists. That is a question of *distribution* of the value created in production. But it is in the *production* of value that Marx finds the key contradiction of the capitalist mode of production: namely between the productivity of labour and the profitability of capital.

Portes says, because Marx got it wrong when he thought wages would be driven to subsistence levels, *"in turn, Marx's most important prediction – that an inevitable conflict between workers and capitalists would lead ultimately to the victory of the former and the end of capitalism – was wrong."* He goes on to argue that *"thanks to increased productivity, workers' demands in most advanced capitalist economies could be satisfied without the system collapsing."* Well, the system may not have 'collapsed', but it is subject to regular and recurring crises of production, and sometimes long periods of economic depression that sap the incomes, employment and future of billions. And have *"workers demands in most advanced capitalist economies"* (Portes leaves out the billions in other economies, just as Keynes did) been *"satisfied"*? What about the poverty levels in most advanced economies, what about employment conditions, housing, education and health? What about huge and increasing levels of inequality of wealth and income in 'most advanced capitalist economies', let alone globally?

Portes admits that there was huge inequality *"in the late 19th and early 20th centuries"*. However, *"not only did this trend stop in the 20th century, it was sharply reversed … after the Second World War the welfare state redistributed income and wealth within the framework of a capitalist economy."* But this 'golden era' of reduced inequality was a short-lived exception, something that the work of Thomas Piketty and others have shown.[95] Portes knows that after the 1970s inequality rose again but he accepts the argument that *"the chief story of the past quarter-century has been the rise of the "middle class": people in emerging economies who have incomes of up to $5,000 a year."* Actually, the reduced level of 'global inequality' between countries and between income groups is down solely to the ending of poverty for 600m people in China. Exclude China and global inequality of wealth and income is no better, if not worse, than 50 years ago. Capitalism has not been a success here.

For Portes, what is wrong with capitalism is not its failure to eliminate poverty or inequality or meet the basic needs of billions in peace and security, as Marx argued. No, it is excessive consumption. *"Although we are at least twice as rich as we were half a century ago, the urge to consume more seems no less strong.… we strive to "keep up with the Joneses".* But excessive or endemic 'consumerism' is not an issue for the billions in the world or even millions in the UK, Europe or the US – it's the opposite: the lack of consumption, including 'social goods' (public services, health, education, pensions, social care etc).

Portes does recognise that capitalism is not harmoniously dynamic and that it has crises. However, apparently all that is necessary is to regulate the financial sector properly and all will be well. He *"would prefer a more wholesale approach to reining in the financial system; this would have gained the approval of Keynes, who thought that while finance was necessary, its role in capitalism should be strictly limited."* But what if *"there is a more fundamental problem: that recurrent crises are baked into the system?"* Then we need to *"make sure that we have better contingency plans next time round."* But is the explanation of crises under capitalism that go back 160 years or more to be found in the lack of regulation of finance? Marx had more to say on this with his law of profitability and the role of fictitious capital. And if Marx was right, 'better contingency plans' to 'regulate' finance will not be (and have not been) enough to avoid more slumps.

Portes finishes by saying that *"There is no viable economic alternative to capitalism at the moment but that does not mean one won't emerge."* But he is vague: *"The defining characteristic of the economy and society will be how that is produced, owned and commanded: by the state, by individuals, by corporations, or in some way as yet undefined."* Indeed *"just as it wasn't the "free market" or individual capitalists who freed the slaves, gave votes to women and created the welfare state, it will be the collective efforts of us all that will enable humanity to turn economic advances into social progress."* Portes is implying the need for socialism, namely a collectively-owned and democratically-run economy of super-abundance that eventually ends the 'economic question' itself. That was Marx's vision too – but it would only be possible by the ending of the capitalist mode of production, not by 'regulating' it.

Mainstream economics was so baffled by the current crisis, that some of them were forced to look at Marx for help. But there is an ignorance of Marxist ideas and, above all, an ideological desire to dismiss them as soon as they are raised. These mainstream commentators on Marx emphasise his ethical or moral objections to capitalism. That's because they don't want to admit that there is anything in the capitalist mode of production that is faulty as a mechanism for meeting human needs. But it is just that criticism that Marx makes, as well as the 'moral' one.

Marx's law of value: the so-called transformation problem
In the early 1970s leading Keynesian Paul Samuelson[96] launched an attack on the validity and purpose of Marx's value theory, as it began to gain some traction among student activists in those 'revolutionary' days.[97]

Like Eugene Bohm-Bawerk tried to do in the late 1890s,[98] and like Keynes in the 1930s, Samuelson wanted to expose the fallacies of Marx's theory in case economics students became 'infected' with Marxism. Keynes had called Marx's value theory *"scientifically erroneous and without application to the modern world"*[99]. Samuelson's approach was to argue, not that Marx's value theory was illogical because values when measured in labour time could not equal prices measured in markets (as

Bohm-Bawerk claimed), but that his theory of value was *irrelevant* to an explanation of the movement of market prices and therefore to any understanding of modern economies.

Samuelson argued that Marx's 'transformation' of labour values into prices of production was unnecessary. Market prices are explained by the movement of supply and demand, so what need of a value theory? Indeed, it could be erased. *"The truth has now been laid bare. Stripped of logical complication and confusion, anybody's method of solving the famous transformation problem is seen to involve returning from an unnecessary detour... such a transformation is precisely like that which an eraser is used to rub out an earlier entry* (i.e. value – MR) *after which we make a new start to end up with a properly calculated entry* (i.e. price – MR)".

William Baumol, a leading neoclassical economist at the time, came to Marx's rescue[100]. Baumol pointed out that Samuelson, along with post-Keynesian Marxists like Joan Robinson, misunderstood Marx's purpose in the so-called transformation of values into prices. Marx did not want to show that market prices were related directly to values measured in labour time. *"Marx did not intend his transformation analysis to show how prices can be* deduced *from values".* The aim was to show that capitalism was a mode of production for profit and profits came from the exploitation of labour; but this fact was obscured by the market where things seemed to be exchanged on the basis of an equality of supply and demand. For Marx, profit first comes from the exploitation of labour and then is redistributed (transformed) among the branches of capital through competition and the market into prices of production.

For Marx, that only labour creates value was self-evident.[101] Total surplus value is produced from exploitation of work forces employed by various capitalists – the difference in value measured in labour time between that time needed for the wages of the labour force and the price of the commodity or service produced realised in the market place for the capitalist. But the surplus value or profit achieved by each capitalist's workforce does not go directly to the individual capitalist. Each capitalist competes in the market to sell its commodities. And that competition leads to profits being redistributed because profits tend to an average rate per unit of capital invested. The transformation of values created by labour into prices in the market means that individual prices will differ from individual values. As Baumol said, Marx knew that individual prices of production differed from individual values; unlike Ricardo who could not solve this transformation.

So total surplus value is converted (transformed) into profit, interest and rent, with the market deciding how much goes to each capitalist. Yes, 'supply and demand' decides profit or loss for an individual capitalist. But that is just the appearance or result of the distribution of profit through market competition but created by the overall exploitation of labour in the production process.

Baumol's explanation was a starting point for a more comprehensive answer and defence of Marx's value theory developed by Marxist scholars like Carchedi, Yaffe, Kliman, Freeman,[102] Moseley and others over the last 40 years since Samuelson's attack. Baumol's interpretation of Marx's theory provides a powerful answer not only to Samuelson but also to the 'standard interpretation' of the transformation problem, as Fred Moseley has named it in his book, Money and Totality[103] (a book that explains in detail all the theoretical issues raised by mainstream and other heterodox economists and answers them).

Values in a commodity do not have to be 'transformed' into prices, as Robinson and Samuelson interpret Marx's theory. Prices are the appearance in the market of the exploitation of labour in the production process. As Moseley says, if you accept Samuelson's interpretation of Marx's transformation of values into prices, then *"values do in fact cancel out and play no role in the determination of prices"*[104]. However, this is not Marx's theory. Individual values are not converted into individual prices of production: *"individual values play no role in Marx's theory of prices*. What happens is that *"total new value produced by current labour ... is determined (in part) by the total surplus value produced, which in turn (in part) determines the general rate of profit and ultimately, prices of production... prices of production are not determined by multiplying transformation coefficients for each commodity by the individual values, but by adding the average profit to given money costs"*.

There is no need to transform the values of constant capital (machinery etc) and variable capital (labour power/workforce) into prices. They are already given as prices from the market in the previous process of production. The only transformation that takes place is the transformation of the total <u>new</u> value from the production process in a re-distribution through market competition, with profits going to the various capitalists depending on the size of capital each advanced at the start of production. As Baumol said, the distribution of surplus value from society's central storehouse now takes place via the competitive process which assigns to each capital profits (or interest or rent) an amount strictly proportional to its capital investment. *"This is the heart of the transformation process – the conversion of surplus value into profit, interest and rent. It takes from each according to its workforce and returns to each according to its total investment."*

Marx's transformation is temporal: you start with given money capital to invest in plant, machinery and labour (t1) and you get new value created by the exertion and exploitation of labour (t2). The surplus value comes after covering the cost of capital (constant and variable). This is then redistributed through competition in the market, which drives all towards an average rate of profit. Thus total value (dead labour and living labour plus surplus value) still equals total prices (based on the given cost of invested capital plus an average rate of profit), but total surplus value is transformed into profits, interest and rent and distributed according to the size of the capital invested.

Here is Marx's actual schema for this transformation.

The transformation
Relative prices are determined by the cost of capital advanced in the production period plus an average rate of profit (ARP) as reached through competition among capitals

Sectors	c	v	s	Total Value	_	c	v	p	Total Price
1	80	20	20	120		80	20	49	149
2	60	30	30	120		60	30	44	134
3	50	40	40	130		50	40	44	134
4	40	70	70	180		40	70	54	164
5	20	80	80	180		20	80	49	149
Total	250	240	240	730		250	240	240	730

You can see that total values (TV =730) equal total prices (TP =730), but individual capitals have commodities with different values (TV) to prices (TP) because of the redistribution of surplus value (s) into profits (p) by the market. There is no transformation of constant (c) and variable (v) capitals, because they are already transformed (into money prices) in the *previous* production period.

Indeed, Marx's transformation has since been supported empirically. Carchedi has shown that the money price average rate of profit is close to the value average rate of profit (i.e. across a whole economy).[105] Other scholars have shown that when an individual sector's production is measured in value terms (i.e. in labour time) and then aggregated, the total value is pretty close to total prices measured in money terms.[106] Thus Marx's transformation of value into prices is not irrelevant even to relative price determination.

But, as Baumol said, it was not Marx's purpose to show that. He wanted to show that it is the exploitation of labour that creates value (through the private appropriation of the product of labour power) and that lies behind profit, interest and rent. Profit is not the reward for 'risking capital' (money for equipment etc); or rent from 'providing' land; or interest for 'lending' money ie 'rewards' to various 'factors of production'. Baumol comments: *"Such nonsense is precisely what Marx' analysis anticipates and what it is intended to expose."* [107]

Marx's law of value: two sources of profit?
Marx was very appreciative of classical economists Smith and Ricardo's objective insights into the nature of industrial capitalism. But he had profound disagreements and criticisms of their labour theory of value, which failed to recognise the dual nature of commodity production – combining use value (output of things and services) and exchange value (pricing in the capitalist market). That dual nature reveals: first, that it is labour (power) that creates value; and second, that profit is the result of the exploitation of labour.

Moreover, competition in the market place means there is a tendency to equalise profit rates between sectors and industries as the result of capital flows searching for the highest profit. So, as Marx explained, market prices move around (ever-changing) prices of production (measured as the cost of capital plus an average rate of profit) not around individual values of commodities measured by the labour time in them. This was Ricardo's omission or error in his labour theory of value.

This difference is crucial because Marx's theory of value shows that it is the exploitation of labour as a commodity that is at the heart of the capitalist mode of production and that the competitive struggle between capital for the share of the surplus value appropriated from labour power leads not only to a tendency to equalise profit rates, but also to a tendency for the average rate of profit to fall. This is the result of capitalist competition and the drive to reduce the value of labour power in total value.

This is the fundamental contradiction in the capitalist mode of production and it is Marx's theory, not Ricardo's or Smith's. Both the latter recognised that the rate of profit in an economy fell but neither Ricardo nor Smith reckoned this was due to the exploitative role of capital over labour or the unintended result of the capitalist drive for more profit. Their 'dismal' explanation for a falling rate of profit was either rising wage costs (Ricardo) or intense competition (Smith). The Ricardian answer of rising input costs was followed by the 20th century neo-Ricardians like Piero Sraffa[108] or the post-Keynesians like Joan Robinson[109] and Michal Kalecki[110] – in opposition to Marx's value theory and law of profitability. Their positions cannot be reconciled with Marx – and more important, are not correct.

The key point here is that profit has only one source: the exploitation of labour and surplus value. This differs from James Steuart, the classical economist[111] who talked about two sources of profit: *positive* profit from production and *relative* profit from transfers of value from one capital to another. Marx did not agree that extra value is also created by trade and not just production. Marx says *"Before the Physiocrats, surplus-value — that is, profit in the form of profit — was explained purely from exchange, the sale of the commodity above its value. Sir James Steuart on the whole did not get beyond this restricted view; (but) he must rather be regarded as the man who reproduced it in scientific form. I say "in scientific form". For Steuart does not share the illusion that the surplus-value which accrues to the individual capitalist from selling the commodity above its value is a creation of new wealth."*

And Marx goes on: *"This profit upon alienation therefore arises from the price of the goods being greater than their real value, or from the goods being sold above their value. Gain on the one side therefore always involves loss on the other. No addition to the general stock is created." But "his theory of "vibration of the balance of wealth between parties", however little it touches the nature and origin of surplus-value itself, remains important in considering the distribution of surplus-value among different classes and among different categories such as profit, interest and rent. (my emphasis)."* So there is no new profit from trade or transfer. This relative profit is just that, relative.

But some critics of Marx's laws want to find new value from outside the exploitation of labour in production to explain how finance capital can gain extra profit from outside production. This extra profit comes from 'revenue' (i.e. profit circulating or hoarded and now outside production). Just as a burglar can gain profit from stealing and selling on, so can a banker from extorting extra interest and fees from workers savings and mortgages. This source of profit is sometimes called 'accumulation by dispossession'[112] or 'profit without producing'.[113]

Now finance capital can gain profit from slicing off a bit of workers' wages in bank interest or from squeezing the 'profit of enterprise' (non-financial capital). But this is not an extra source of profit but merely a redistribution of surplus value or a reduction of the value of labour power. It does not mean that finance capital 'creates' a new source in the circulation of capital. Profit can be gained from 'unequal exchange', say with poor parts of the 'non-capitalist' world. But taking hides and gold from the New World off indigenous tribes for little or nothing is not a new source of value; it is the (pre-capitalist) exploitation of the labour of those peoples.

As Joseph Choonara has pointed out[114]: *"exploitation in a Marxist sense has a quite specific meaning. It relates to the extraction of surplus value from workers even though the commodity they supply, their labour power, is obtained by the capitalist at its value. The surplus value generated is not a "swindle" as pre-Marxist socialists had argued but a result of the gap between the new value created by labour over a given period of time and the value required to reproduce that labour power (the wage). The mechanisms associated with financialisation do not generate surplus value.*

As anyone with an overdraft can testify, it is undeniable that banks make profit out of personal finance. To the extent that wages rise to account for this, it is a mechanism that shifts surplus value from capitalists concerned with production to those concerned with lending money, just as an arbitrary rise in the price of bread would (if wages rose correspondingly) shift surplus value to bread-producing capitalists. To the extent that wages are held down, it represents an increase in overall exploitation of workers, just as an arbitrary rise in food prices would under conditions of wage repression. And to the extent that workers default on their debts, whether credit cards or subprime mortgages, it represents a decline in a market in fictitious capital, with banks (and others) holding claims over future wage income, some of which turn out to be worthless. Whatever happens, the generation of surplus value within capitalist enterprises remains central to the system as a whole."

So if the argument is that this is an extra source of profit that must be added into economic accounts, then that breaks with Marxist theory or for that matter even with the 'classical tradition' as suggested by Stueart. It concedes to the ambiguities of modern "financialisation" theories[115] namely that it is finance that is now the exploiter, not capital.[116] This attempt to identify sources of profit that are additional to surplus value in the exploitation of labour in production is *"what left-Keynesian economists, supported by the Keynesian-Marxists, really hope to achieve is to replace profits based on surplus value—that is, exploitation—with profits based on buying low and selling dear and on this basis reconcile the interests of the working class and the capitalist class."*[117]

There is no reconciliation possible between Marx's value theory and that of Ricardo and Sraffa. There is also no unification between Marx's law of profitability as the underlying cause of recurrent crises and slumps with the post Keynesian/Kalecki view of a 'profit-wage share' economy. And there is no meeting between Marx's view of profitability and credit in modern capitalism and those who hold that finance creates value and that 'financial speculation' lies at the centre of capitalist crises.

Marx's law of profitability: correcting Marx

In 2014, French mainstream economist, Thomas Piketty published a huge book, which subsequently became a best seller as leading mainstream economists in the US gave it rave reviews. It became the best-selling book that was never read, replacing <u>A Brief History of Time</u> by physicist Stephen Hawking for that honour. The title of Piketty's book, <u>Capital in the 21ˢᵗ century</u>[118] was a clear allusion by him to Karl Marx's book of the same name, Capital. Piketty was suggesting that he was updating (and indeed correcting) Marx's analysis of 19ᵗʰ century capitalism for the 21ˢᵗ century.

According to Piketty, Marx needed correcting because, despite his clever intuition that *"private capital accumulation could lead to the concentration of wealth in ever fewer hands"*, he got the whole mechanism for this development totally wrong. Marx thought that capitalism would have an *"apocalyptic"* end but thanks to *"modern economic growth and the diffusion of knowledge"* that has been avoided. But there is still the problem of the *"deep structures of capital inequality"*.

Piketty goes on: the basis of Marx's prediction of an apocalyptic end to capitalism was *"either the rate of return on capital would steadily diminish (thereby killing the engine of accumulation and leading to violent conflict among capitalists) or capital's share of national income would increase indefinitely until the workers went into revolt."* Marx reckoned that wages would be stagnant or falling. This was wrong because *"like his predecessors Marx totally neglected the possibility of durable technological progress and steadily increasing productivity, which is a force that can to some extent serve as a counterweight to the process of accumulation and concentration of capital"*. Unfortunately, you see, Marx failed to use the stats available in the 19ᵗʰ century and *"devoted little thought"* to how a non-capitalist society might work. If he had done so, he might have sorted out his mistakes.

Already, it will be clear to a student of Marx's analysis of a capitalist economy that Piketty is unaware that Marx saw the drive to raise the productivity of labour through technological advance the flipside of the accumulation of capital – Marx's law of accumulation (see chapter 2). Instead, Piketty adopts the neoclassical distortion that Marx's theory is based on an 'iron law of wages' and a zero rise in productivity: *"Marx's theory implicitly relies on a strict assumption of zero productivity growth over the long run"*. This is not surprising when we learn that Piketty admits that he has never read the very book that carries the same name as his. *"I never managed really to read it. I mean I don't know if you've tried to read it. Have you tried?... The Communist Manifesto of 1848 is a short and strong piece. Das Kapital, I think, is very difficult to read and for me it was not very influential.... The big difference is that my book is a book about the history of capital. In the books of Marx there's no data."*

But no matter, let us consider Piketty's *'superior analysis'* of the laws of motion of capitalism in the 21st century. To do that, we must first consider Piketty's definition of capital. For Piketty, *"Capital is defined as the sum total of nonhuman assets that can be owned and exchanged on some market. Capital includes all forms of real property (including residential real estate) as well as financial and professional capital (plants, infrastructure, machinery, patents and so on) used by* firms and government agencies." In effect, for Piketty, capital and wealth (mainly personal wealth) are the same. *"To simplify the test, I use the word capital and wealth interchangeably as if they were perfectly synonymous".*

This is different from capital as defined by Marx. For Marx, capital is a social relation specific to the capitalist mode of production. It is self-expanding value. Value comes from the exertion of labour and is realised on a market. It is measured in labour time (and in its monetary expression). Under the capitalist mode of production, the owners of the means of production put workers and machinery to work to produce things or services that people need (use values) but they only do so if value is also created (specifically, surplus value).

Under the capitalist mode of production, things and services that people need are produced simply as a money-making exercise, but this money comes from value created by the exertion of labour power, with the surplus over and above the living needs of labour appropriated by the owners of capital. Thus the circuit of capital, for Marx, is M-C...P...C1 to M1, namely capitalists have money capital (M) which is invested in commodities (C), means of production and raw materials, which are used by labour in production (P) to produce commodities (C1) for sale on the market for more money (M1). Capital (M) expands value to accumulate more capital (M1). But only labour created that new value.

With Piketty, this process and its social relation are ignored. Capital is wealth and wealth is capital. Wealth existed before the capitalist mode of production became dominant in the world, so wealth is not specific to capitalism. Indeed, wealth is really a measure of accumulated assets, tangible and financial. Wealth/capital is in all societies. So for Piketty, the capital process is M…M1. Money accumulates more money (or wealth). It does not matter how and so there is no need to define capital as different from wealth.

This is what Marx called 'vulgar economics', i.e. failing to see the underlying process of accumulation and just observing the appearance – indeed seeing things from the view of the holder of wealth. As he says, in the novels of Jane Austen or Balzac, all the characters who are holders of wealth live off the income from that wealth. All they were interested in was the return on that wealth, not how it was generated (whether by slaves, land rents or interest on consols).

Piketty specifically rules out the approach of the classical economists and Marx: *"Some definitions of capital hold that the term should apply only to those components of wealth directly employed in the production process… this limitation strikes me as neither desirable nor practical."* So *"I ruled out the idea of excluding residential real estate from capital on the grounds that it is 'unproductive' unlike productive capital used by firms and governments… the truth is that all these forms of wealth are useful and productive and reflect capital's two major economic functions"*.

Well, residential property is obviously useful to the user. It has use-value as Marx would say. But this form of wealth is not productive of new value (or profit), unless it is owned by a real estate company which rents it out as a business. Nevertheless, Piketty concocts a way for this wealth to deliver income: *"residential real estate can be seen as a capital asset that yields 'housing services' whose value is measure by their rental equivalent."*

Now Piketty might say: does this distinction matter? For Piketty, it does not, because income is income and wealth is wealth wherever it comes from. But it does matter if we are to understand better the laws of motion of capitalism. By including residential property, net financial assets and land in his definition of capital, Piketty reaches opposite conclusions from Marx on the return on capital, or what Marx called the rate of profit. And that matters. For a start, it means that Piketty is interested in the distribution of wealth and not on how it is generated. For him, the former provides the key contradiction of capitalism, while for Marx it is the latter.

This brings us to what Piketty designates grandiosely as *"the first fundamental law of capitalism"*, namely that the capital/income ratio β is related to the capital share of income α, where r is the net rate of return on capital. This is an accounting identity. $α = r \times β$. Capital's share of national income α is equal to the capital income ratio β in an economy times the net rate of return on capital, r. So inequality of wealth, as expressed by capital's share of income, will rise if the rate of return on the existing wealth ratio (the capital income ratio) rises. Alternatively, the wealth ratio will rise, if capital's share of national income rises.

Piketty's r is central to this simple but illuminating analysis. And for him, his r is better than Marx's. As he says: *"the rate of return on capital is a central concept in many economic theories. In particular, Marxist analysis emphasises the falling rate of profit – a historical prediction that has turned out to be quite wrong, although it does contain an interesting intuition."* His net rate of return is a *"broader"* notion than the rate of profit as it incorporates interest, rent etc as well as profit. Piketty does not realise that Marx's rate of profit (as surplus value divided by capital) is just as broad because surplus value is divided into (not composed of) rent, interest and profit too.

However, argues Piketty, Marx was wrong to reckon that r would fall over time and this would cause recurrent crises. Instead, Piketty tells us that actually r does not fall over time but rises or at least stays pretty steady. So the issue for 21st century capitalism is that: if r grows faster than g (net real national income growth), then capital's share of income will grow and the global capital/income ratio will eventually reach unsustainable levels. The crisis of capitalism is thus one of *"terrifying"* social instability, not one of contradictions within the capitalist mode of production.

Indeed, there is little or nothing in Piketty's 685 pages about booms and slumps, or about the Great Depression, the Great Recession, or other recessions, except to say that the Great Recession was a 'financial panic' (as claimed by Ben Bernanke) and was not as bad as the Great Depression because of the intervention of the central banks and the state. There is nothing about the waste of production, jobs and incomes. Piketty adopts the usual neoclassical explanation that these events, like wars, were exogenous 'shocks' to the long-term expansion of productivity and economic growth under capitalism. Crises are just short-term shocks and we can revert to his fundamental law instead *"as it allows us to understand the potential equilibrium level toward which the capital income ratio tend in the long run when the effects of shocks and crises have dissipated".*

Piketty argues that Marx's r falls because in his model of capitalism, there is *"an infinite accumulation of capital"* and *"as ever more increasing quantities of capital lead inexorably to a falling rate of profit (i.e. return on capital) and eventually to their own downfall, while growth in net income (g) falls to zero."* Here Piketty imposes a marginal productivity theory of capital accumulation on Marx; abundance of capital leads to its diminishing returns. Actually, Marx rejected this scarcity theory. For Marx, the movement in r is to be found not in infinite accumulation but in the rise in value of the means of production relative to the value of labour power. Piketty says that after World War 2, capital was scarce and so the return on capital was high. Marx would have said capital values had been destroyed (both physically and in value) so the rate of profit was high. It was not scarcity of 'capital'.

We can even check if Marx's law of the tendency of the rate of profit to fall bears out in reality over the long run. Maito estimates the Marxian rate of profit in 14 countries in the long run going back to 1870, using national historical data for each country[119]. His results show a clear downward trend in the world rate of profit, although there are periods of partial recovery. There is a secular tendency for the rate of profit to fall under capitalism and Marx's law operates. Maito also uses Piketty's historical data for Germany to get a rate of profit for that economy. Unlike Piketty, Maito leaves out residential property and correctly categorises capital as the value of the means of production owned and accumulated in the capitalist sector. The result is not some steady r, but a falling rate of profit *a la* Marx. There is a long-term decline, but with a rise from the 1980s to 2007. Actually, Piketty's r for Germany also falls from 1950 and then stabilises from the 1980s too. This is because Germans generally have a much lower ownership of residential property. Only 44% of German households own their own homes, compared with 70-80% in Greece, Italy and Spain.

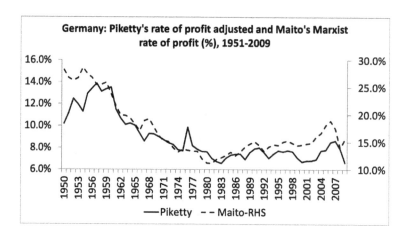

Is it a tendency for a rising net return on capital (Piketty) or is it the tendency for a falling rate of profit (Marx) that is the key contradiction of capitalism in the 21st century? If it is the former, then all we need to do is to introduce a progressive tax system. We don't need to bury capitalism, as we can save it. But if it is the latter, then the main contradiction in the capitalist mode of production would not be resolved. There would be recurring slumps in investment and output, huge increases in unemployment and losses in wage income and even a descent into long depressions. The solution then is one of replacing the capitalist mode of production.

The Keynesian critique: "scientifically erroneous and without application to the modern world" (Keynes)

In 1926, John Maynard Keynes, already the most celebrated economist and political writer of his time, reviewed the competing ideas of conventional economics (which he called 'laisser-faire') and its revolutionary alternative (Marxism). In his book, Laisser-faire and Communism, Keynes, a contemporary of the Bolshevik leaders Lenin and Trotsky, sought to dismiss the Soviet revolution that had shocked the ruling groups of the rest of the world just a few years before.

His attack was that: how could anything worthwhile come out of communism, based as it was on the ideas and theories of Karl Marx? *"How can I accept the [Communist] doctrine,"* Keynes wrote, *"which sets up as its bible, above and beyond criticism, an obsolete textbook which I know not only to be scientifically erroneous but without interest or application to the modern world?"* And more: *"Even if we need a religion, how can we find it in the turbid rubbish of the red bookshop? It is hard for an educated, decent, intelligent son of Western Europe to find his ideals here, unless he has first suffered some strange and horrid process of conversion which has changed all his values."*[120]

For him, Marxism was to be condemned for *"exalting the boorish proletariat above the bourgeoisie and the intelligentsia, who are the quality in life and carry the seeds of all human advancement"*. He saw Marxism as a product of a combination of (quote) *'jewish and russian natures'*. And for him, that was bad. Keynes was an upper class snob with all the class prejudices. He refused to support the Labour party in the 1930s, siding with the Liberals because Labour was *"a class party and that class is not my class."*

In Laisser-faire and Communism, Keynes concluded: *"For the most part, I think that Capitalism, wisely managed, can probably be made more efficient for attaining economic ends than any alternative system yet in sight";* while Socialism *"is, in fact, little better than a dusty survival of a plan to meet the problems of fifty years ago, based on a misunderstanding of what someone said a hundred years ago."*

In contrast, to Marx's 'illogical and obsolete' labour theory of value, Keynes accepted the mainstream marginal utility theory. When this became the dominant explanation for prices of production in an economy, replacing the labour theory in the late 1870s, Engels remarked: *"The fashionable theory just now here is that of Stanley Jevons, according to which value is determined by utility and on the other hand by the limit of supply (i.e. the cost of production), which is merely a confused and circuitous way of saying that value is determined by supply and demand. Vulgar Economy everywhere!"* [121] Marginal utility theory quickly became untenable even in mainstream circles because subjective value cannot be measured and aggregated, so the psychological foundation of marginal utility was soon given up, but without abandoning the theory itself. Thus Keynes continued to hold to a scientifically erroneous theory of prices, which was untestable while rubbishing Marx's objective and testable theory of value based on labour time expended.

Keynes also had a theory of declining profitability. In the General Theory, you find him raising the idea of profitability pretty early. He calls profitability 'the marginal efficiency of capital', using neoclassical terminology from the concept of 'factors of production'. So profit is the return on the 'factor' of capital, just as wages are the return on the factor of labour. Keynes tells us that *"the predominant explanation of crisis is not primarily a rise in the rate of interest, but a sudden collapse in the marginal efficiency of capital"*.

But he saw the decline of the rate of profit not as pointing toward a revolutionary transformation in the mode of production, but rather as representing a progressive *"softening in the antagonism"* between the capitalists and the working class. As capital becomes *"less scarce"* relative to labour, the rate of profit will fall and real wages will rise. More of the total product will therefore go to the working class and less will go to the capitalists – inequality would decline.

As the *"scarcity-value"* of capital dissipated, according to Keynes, economic growth would peter out. Interest rates would fall to zero or very close to zero, causing the gradual extinction of the hateful *"money capitalists."* This would leave the industrial and commercial capitalists able to earn a little extra profit by taking on *"entrepreneurial"* risks. Wages up, profits up - in a 'stationary' world of superabundance.

In his major work, The General Theory, Keynes quickly drops his long term analysis of profitability and moves on to more short-term fluctuations in the monetary sector (for Marx, the whole economy is monetary). What causes a crisis is when entrepreneurs are over-optimistic about potential profit relative to the going rate of interest. So the problem is not the rate of profit as such, but unpredictable expectations that it will be high enough to justify the going rate of interest. When it is not, then a crisis can ensue. The crisis is a product of wrong judgements, not the actual rate of profit relative to the needed reproduction of capital, as Marx would argue. The marginal efficiency of capital properly expresses the return on that factor of production as it tends to an equilibrium. So there is nothing wrong with the production process under capitalism. The problem is in the financial sector where the rate of interest gets out of line.

Keynes' important contribution was in recognising that capitalism cannot sustain full employment. For him, high unemployment was not a temporary aberration in the smooth running of capitalist production as the economic orthodoxy said at the time. No, unemployment could well set in for a long time. It was the product of a failure within 'capitalism', or what he preferred to call, a 'modern economy'. For Keynes, in so far as capitalism could not deliver on full employment and dropped into crises and slumps and even long depressions, the culprit was not Capital as such but the financial sector and the cause was in the monetary nature of the economy, not its capitalist nature. According to Keynes, a crisis and slump comes about when suddenly there is a change of 'animal spirits' among the holders of money. They no longer want to lend money for investment or consumption. Instead, they start to hoard it. Thus a lack of 'effective demand' emerges in the economy. With the drying up of funds for investing or spending in the shops, investment and consumption drops and employment falls.

Keynes' special explanation of this is that this situation could last indefinitely because holders of cash or lenders of credit will prefer to keep their money liquid. They have extreme 'liquidity preference' and the economy goes into a 'liquidity trap'. Thus the state and the central bank must intervene to kick-start the economy again with easy or cheap money or outright government spending to compensate for the private sector drying up. It might even be necessary to 'socialise' investment (ie boost public investment) to get it going. A determined government policy in the short term can thus end the depression, restore 'animal spirits' and get the productive sector of the capitalist system back into action again. Then all will be well.

Actually, Keynes himself was not on the side of the workers in a solution to a slump. *"In emphasising our point of departure from the classical system, we must not overlook an important point of agreement. ... with a given organisation, equipment and technique, real wages and the volume of output (and hence of employment) are uniquely correlated, so that, in general, an increase in employment can only occur to the accompaniment of a decline in the rate of real wages. Thus I am not disputing this vital fact which the classical economists have (rightly) asserted as indefeasible."* So cutting real wages was part of the solution to a slump for Keynes, just as it was with neoclassical mainstream economics.

97

The trouble with Keynes is that he was so inconsistent in his ideas that it becomes even more difficult to follow just what his theory and views are than it does with Marx! Keynes was a dynamic personality and a great writer on current events (as was Marx) but his General Theory makes Marx's Capital seem like a model of simplicity. Keynes answered his arch rival, the Austrian economist Hayek, who complained that he kept changing his views[122] by saying that *'if the facts change, I change my ideas, don't you?'* But it does not help if somebody changes ideas like changing shirts. Sometimes Keynes seems to be saying that the answer to depression is easy money and low interest rates; at other times, he argues that is not enough and you need government spending and budget deficits; and then later he argues that budget deficits are bad. Sometimes he advocated the 'socialisation of investment' implying replacing capitalist investment, but at other times, he wants private capital protected.

Indeed, towards the end of his life in the postwar period he seemed to suggest that his radical policies of easy money and government deficit were not necessarily right. *"I must not be misunderstood. I do not suppose that the (neo) classical medicine will work by itself or that we can depend on it. We need quicker and less painful aids. . . . But in the long run, these expedients will work better and we shall need them less, if the classical medicine is also at work. And if we reject the medicine from our systems altogether, we may just drift on from expedient to expedient and never get really fit again."*[123]

In 1931, at the depth of the Great Depression, Keynes told his students at Cambridge University, many of whom were becoming attracted to the 'obsolete' theories of Marx that they should not worry. The Great Depression would pass: it was a 'technical problem' that could be corrected. *"I draw the conclusion that, assuming no important wars and no important increase in population, the economic problem may be solved, or be at least within sight of solution, within a hundred years. This means that the economic problem is not – if we look into the future – the permanent problem of the human race."* The long-term future under capitalism through an expansion of technology, and assuming no more wars (!) and population control, would be a world of leisure with a 15-hour week and superabundance for all, well before Marx's 200th anniversary.

The evidence since Keynes dismissed Marx's theories is that, far from finance capital being consigned to history, finance capital has never been more powerful globally; and inequality of wealth and incomes within national economies and globally has never been more extreme since capitalism became the dominant mode of production. Also, most people in the Western world are still working 40-hour weeks and the level of poverty within 'rich' modern economies is still high. In the rest of the world, unemployment, sweated labour and poverty are the modal experience. No world of leisure there.

Marx versus Keynes/Kalecki: the theory of crises

Investment (especially business investment) is the key driver of economic growth and the main swing factor in the capitalist business cycle of boom and slump.[124] The Keynesian macro-identities suggest that investment drives GDP, employment and profits through the mechanism of effective demand. But Marxist theory says that it is profit that 'calls the tune', not investment. Profit is part of surplus value, or the unpaid labour in production. It is the result of the exploitation of labour – something ignored or denied by Keynesian theory, where profit is the result of 'capital' as a factor of production.

If we analyse the changes in investment and consumption prior to each recession or slump in the post-war US economy, we find that consumption demand has played little or no leading role in provoking a slump. In the six recessions since 1945, US personal consumption fell less than GDP or investment on every occasion and did not fall at all in 1980-2. Investment fell by 8-30% on every occasion. If investment is the driver of growth or the 'swing factor' in recession, the question is what causes investment to rise and fall? Keynesian theory does not ignore investment as a key factor in the movement of economic activity. It considers the question using macro-identities.

Let us consider these identities. We start with:

National income = national expenditure.

National income can then be broken down to Profit + Wages;

National expenditure can be broken down to Investment + Consumption.

So Profit + Wages = Investment + Consumption.

Now if we assume that wages are all spent on consumption and not saved, then

Profits = Investment.

But this identity does not tell us the causal direction that can help us develop a theory of what moves economies and/or a theory of crises.

For Keynesians, the causal direction is that investment creates profit. For orthodox Keynesians, crises come about because of a collapse in aggregate or 'effective demand' in the economy (as expressed in a fall of investment and consumption). This fall in investment leads to a fall in employment and thus to less income. Effective demand is the independent variable and incomes and employment are the dependent variables. There is no mention of profit or profitability in this causal schema.

Nevertheless, Keynes understood the central role of profit in the capitalist system. *"Unemployment, I must repeat, exists because employers have been deprived of profit. The loss of profit may be due to all sorts of causes. But, short of going over to Communism, there is no possible means of curing unemployment except by restoring to employers a proper margin of profit."*[125] But investment creates profits not vice versa. *"Nothing obviously, can restore employment which does not first restore business profits. Yet nothing, in my judgement, can restore business profits that does not first restore the volume of investment."*[126] To use the pithy phrase of Hyman Minsky, devoted follower of Keynes, *"it is investment that calls the tune".*[127]

Let us return to the macro profit equation outlined above, but now as developed by Michel Kalecki, a Polish economist and synthesiser of Marx and Keynes. His equation is simply that: Profits = Investment; or more importantly, profits <u>depend</u> on investment. As a recent paper by James Montier[128] succinctly put it: *"This is, of course, an identity – a truism by construction. However it can be interpreted with some causality imposed."* Montier goes on: *"Investment drives profits because when a firm or a household decides to invest in some real asset they are effectively buying a good from another firm, creating profits for that entity."* So it seems that profits are a 'residual' and come from consumers buying things or services and not from surplus value created in the labour process, as Marx argued.

This argument is spelt out even more explicitly, by the Jerome Levy Forecasting Center[129]. The authors state that the profits equation identifies the *"sources of profits = investment, non-business saving (households), dividends and profit taxes."* First, this suggests that taxes on profits and dividends are a 'source' of profit rather than part of profit. But if we take out taxes and dividends and assume workers don't save, we are back to the 'source' of profit as investment. *"After all, profits are a residual; they are the remainder after the factors of production have been paid. Thus it can comfortably be argued that the left-hand side of the equation is determined by the right-hand side."*

Jose Tapia points out that *"for the whole Keynesian school, investment is the key variable explaining macroeconomic dynamics and leading the cycle."*[130] But if investment is the independent variable, according to Keynes, what causes a fall in investment? For Keynes, it is loss of 'animal spirits' among entrepreneurs, or a 'lack of confidence' in employing funds for investment. As Minsky says, investment is dependent on *"the subjective nature of expectations about the future course of investment, as well as the subjective determination of bankers and their business clients of the appropriate liability structure for the financing of positions in different types of capital assets".*[131] Tapia shows, for the Keynesians, investment depends on the psychology of investors, which changes <u>for no apparent reason</u> into a loss of faith in expected profits. Profits do appear in the Keynes-Kalecki analysis, but *"in Kalecki, the determination is from investment to profits and in the relation there is little room, if any, for reverse causation."*

For Keynes/Kalecki, profit is the marginal product of 'capital', a 'factor of production'. There is no 'exploitation' of labour power involved. Keynes' theory of crisis assumes falling 'marginal productivity' due to the 'abundance of capital' and thus investment depends on the 'marginal efficiency of capital' and 'animal spirits'. *"We have seen above,"* Keynes wrote, *"that marginal efficiency of capital depends, not only on the existing abundance or scarcity of capital-goods and the current cost of production of capital-goods, but also on current expectations as to the future yield of capital-goods. In the case of durable assets it is, therefore, natural and reasonable that expectations of the future should play a dominant part in determining the scale on which new investment is deemed advisable. But, as we have seen, the basis for such expectations is very precarious.*

Being based on shifting and unreliable evidence, they are subject to sudden and violent changes." [132]

As Paul Mattick Snr said, *"what are we to make of an economic theory, which after all claimed to explain some of the fundamental problems of twentieth-century capitalism, which could declare: 'In estimating the prospects of investment, we must have regard, therefore, to the nerves and hysteria and even the digestions and reactions to the weather of those upon whose spontaneous activity it largely depends'?*[133]

What if we turn the causal direction the other way: the Marxist way[134]. Marx's theory of value tells us that all value is created by labour and profit is a product of the exploitation of labour power and its appropriation by capital. Then we have a theory of profit and investment based on an objective causal analysis within a specific form of class society. And now, investment in an economy depends on profits. With Marx, profit is the result of the exploitation of labour (power) and thus is logically prior to investment. But it is also temporally prior. If we adopt a theory that profits cause or lead investment, that 'profits call the tune', not investment, then we can construct a reasonably plausible cycle of profit, investment and economic activity.

Can we offer empirical evidence in support of the Marxist profit-investment nexus? First, there has been a secular fall in the rate of profit in the major capitalist economies and this has not been caused by an "abundance of capital" relative to output, as 'marginalist' Keynesian theory would argue. And there are many studies that show a close correlation between business investment and the profitability of capital.

Mainstream economists, Kothari, Lewellen and Warner, found a close causal correlation between the movement in US business investment and business profitability[135]. Business investment (as a share of assets) declined in tandem with profitability. The authors concluded that ⊠*investment growth is highly predictable, up to 1½ years in advance, using past profits and stock returns but has little connection to interest rates, credit spreads, or stock volatility. Indeed, profits and stock returns swamp the predictive power of other variables proposed in the literature."* They also found that *"Profits show a clear business-cycle pattern and a clear correlation with investment."* They measured the predictive causal correlation between changes in profits, GDP and investment and the Great Recession. They found that *"if investment maintained its historical connection to profit growth, investment was predicted to drop by 14.7%, roughly two-thirds the actual decline of 23.0%."*

My own research found that for the period 2000 to 2013[136], the correlation between changes in the rate of profit and investment was 64%; second, the correlation between the mass of profit and investment was 76%; and third, the correlation between the rate of profit (lagged one year) and the mass of profit was also 76%.

Economists at investment bank, JP Morgan also found that *"at least three-quarters of the investment decline can be thought of as a historically typical drop given the behaviour of profits and GDP at the end of 2008. Problems in the credit markets may have played a role, but the impact on corporate investment is arguably small."* [137]

The Federal Reserve Bank of Cleveland has also found similar results[138]. Economists there found that there was a very high correlation between the movement of business profits, investment and industrial production. Chief economist Ergundor: *"A simple correlation analysis shows that the correlation between the change in corporate profits and the contemporaneous change in industrial production is 54 percent, but the correlation goes up to 66 percent if I use the one-quarter-ahead change in industrial production. Similarly, the correlation between the change in corporate profits and the contemporaneous change in gross domestic private investment is 57 percent, but the correlation goes up to 68 percent if I use the one-quarter-ahead change in investment.*

More formally, a Granger causality test indicates that the quarterly change in profits leads the quarterly change in production by one quarter, but the change in profits is independent of the change in production. A similar relationship applies to the quarterly change in profits and investment. *"Thus, firms seem to adjust their production and investment after seeing a drop in their profits."* The time gap between profits and investment is about three quarters of a year.

Deutsche Bank economists[139] also noted that *"Profit margins always peak in advance of recession. Indeed, there has not been one business cycle in the post-WWII era where this has not been the case. The reason margins are a leading indicator is simple: when corporate profitability declines, a pullback in spending and hiring eventually ensues."* Deutsche goes on: *"the historical data reveals that the average and median lead times between the peak in margins and the onset of recession are nine and eight quarters, respectively".*

Tapia shows that over 251 quarters of US economic activity from 1947, the movement in profits was much more volatile than the movement in wages or even investment.[140] Most important, *"corporate profits stop growing, stagnate and then start falling a few quarters before a recession".* Profits then lead investment and employment out of each recession. In the long expansion of the 1990s, profits started declining long before investment did (profits fell back in 1997 while investment went on growing until 2000, when a crisis ensued). *"In all these cases, profits peaks several quarters before the recession, while investment peaks almost immediately before the recession."* Using regression analysis, Tapia finds that pre-tax profits can explain 44% of all movement in investment, while there is no evidence that investment can explain any movement in profits.

Finally, G Carchedi and I found that the US mass of profits leads business investment and GDP growth into recession and then out of it[141]. Thus, the evidence is overwhelming that profitability is the driver of investment growth and that profits lead investment (and GDP) and not vice versa[142]. The Marxist view is supported empirically.

Let us return to the Keynes-Kalecki macro identity. It can be re-designed as: Investment – (non-capitalist) Savings = Profits. The Keynesian view is that: the lower are non-capitalist savings, the higher is the investment and then the higher the profits. Non-capitalist (domestic) savings can be divided into three parts: savings by households, saving by governments and foreign capitalist savings. If households save more (as they tend to do in a slump) and foreign savings rises (in other words, the national economy's deficit with the rest of the world rises); if government also run budget surpluses and save, then investment will be lower. And if investment calls the tune, then lower investment will mean lower profits (business savings). However, there is a saviour in this equation: government savings, or to be more exact; government dissaving. If government runs up a big budget deficit, in other words, dissaves, it can boost investment and thus profits. So the Keynesian logic goes.

But the Marxist logic is that the causal connection is the opposite. Thus the equation looks like this. Profits + (non-capitalist) Savings = Investment. If we assume profits are fixed or fall in this equation, then investment cannot be increased or will fall, unless other non-capitalist savings are increased to compensate (namely household savings and/ or reduced capitalist consumption or more government saving, not dissaving). This is the opposite of the Keynesian policy conclusion. On this view, more government borrowing will not boost profits, but the opposite – and profits are what matters under capitalism. So government dissaving is a negative for capitalist investment. Government spending will not boost the capitalist economy because it eats into profitability by depriving the capitalist sector of some of its potential profit.

The Keynesian and Marxist multipliers
The multiplier is a device invented by Richard Kahn, Keynes' disciple of the 1930s. It purports to measure the change in real GDP caused by a change in government spending or taxation – in other words, the impact on growth of government fiscal measures. So the Keynesian multiplier measures the impact of more or less spending (demand) on income (GDP). But it does not measure the impact on profitability. And, in the Marxist view, that is crucial to growth under the capitalist mode of production.

Carchedi presents the difference described here as between the Keynesian multiplier (i.e. consumption to investment to national income to profits) and the Marxist multiplier (i.e. profits to investment to income and consumption). Carchedi: *"In the Keynesian multiplier, state induced investments have a positive effect on production and thus on income, spending, and saving.....Profitability plays a subordinate role and the effects on the economy are always apparently positive. In the Marxist multiplier, profitability is central.... The question is whether n rounds of subsequent investments generate a rate of profit higher than, lower than, or equal to the original average rate of profit".[143]*

If the Marxist multiplier is the right way to view the modern economy, then what follows is that government spending and tax increases or cuts must be viewed from whether they boost or reduce profitability. If they do not raise profitability or even reduce it, then any short-term boost to GDP from more government spending will only be at the expense of a lengthier period of low growth and an eventual return to recession. There is no assurance that more spending means more profits – on the contrary. Government investment in infrastructure may boost profitability for those capitalist sectors getting the contracts, but if it is paid for by higher taxes on profits, there is no gain overall. And if it is financed by borrowing, profitability will eventually be constrained by a rising cost of capital.

So which multiplier is the most convincing on the evidence? Tapia looked at the causal connection between US profits, investment and government spending.[144] He found that *"little evidence is found that government spending may stimulate future investment and in this way may pump-prime the economy."* He concluded that *"The Keynesian view that government expenditure may pump-prime the economy by stimulating private investment has very little support in the data, as the net effect of government expending on lagged private investment is either null or negative. Only in the sample 1961-1990 did past government spending appear as enhancing gross investment in the present, though it does not stimulate business investment, and the effect does not appear in other samples so that it does not constitute strong evidence in favor of a pump-priming effect of government spending. This suggests that it is the profitability of capital that is decisive for the recovery or otherwise from an economic recession or depression."*

Carchedi finds that 1) up to the early 1990s rising government expenditure could not stop the fall in the rate of profit in the post-war period and 2) government expenditures rise from the year preceding the crisis to the last crisis years in all post-war recessions (except 1954). So rising government expenditures did not stop slumps and 3) government spending does not 'reboot' the economy.[145] In contrast, there is a significant positive correlation between changes in profitability of capital (net return on the stock of fixed assets) and economic growth for the G6 economies.

There does not seem to be any evidence that bigger government spending or wider budget deficits will lead to faster investment or economic growth over time in capitalist economies. Indeed, the evidence is to the contrary much of time. The Marxist multiplier of profitability and investment seems more convincing.

Marx, Keynes and the labour movement

Keynesian economics dominates on the left in the labour movement. Keynes is the economic hero of those wanting to change the world; to end poverty, inequality and continual losses of incomes and jobs in recurrent crises. In the US, the great gurus of opposition to the neoliberal theories of Chicago school of economics and the policies of Republican politicians are Keynesians. In the UK, the leftish leaders of the Labour party around Jeremy Corbyn and John McDonnell, self-proclaimed socialists, look to Keynesian economists for their policy ideas and analysis. They bring them onto their advisory councils and seminars.

Those graduate students and lecturers involved in Rethinking Economics[146], an international attempt to change the teaching and ideas away from neoclassical theory, are led by Keynesian authors like James Kwak or post-Keynesians like Steve Keen, or Victoria Chick or Frances Coppola. Here the idea that inequality is the enemy, not capitalism as such, dominates the media and the labour movement. This is not to deny the ugly importance of rising inequality[147], but to show that a Marxist view on this does not circulate.

So why do Keynesian ideas continue to dominate? Geoff Mann provides us with an insightful explanation. In a new book, entitled In the Long Run We are all Dead,[148] Mann reckons it is not that Keynesian economics is seen as correct. There have been *"powerful Left critiques of Keynesian economics from which to draw; examples include the work of Paul Mattick, Geoff Pilling and Michael Roberts"*, but Keynesian ideas dominate the labour movement and among those opposed to what Mann calls 'liberal capitalism' for political reasons.

Keynes rules because he offers a third way between socialist revolution and barbarism, i.e. the end of civilisation as we (actually the bourgeois like Keynes) know it. In the 1920s and 1930s, Keynes feared that the 'civilised world' faced Marxist revolution or fascist dictatorship. But socialism as an alternative to the capitalism of the Great Depression could well bring down 'civilisation', delivering instead 'barbarism' – the end of a better world, the collapse of technology and the rule of law, more wars etc. So he aimed to offer the hope that, through some modest fixing of 'liberal capitalism', it would be possible to make capitalism work without the need for socialist revolution. There would be no need to go where the angels of 'civilisation' fear to tread. That was Keynes' narrative.

This appealed (and still appeals) to the leaders of the labour movement and 'liberals' wanting change. Revolution was too risky and we could all go down with it. Mann: *"the Left wants democracy without populism, it wants transformational politics without the risks of transformation; it wants revolution without revolutionaries"*. This fear of revolution, Mann reckons, was first exhibited after the French revolution. That great experiment in bourgeois democracy turned into Robespierre and the terror; democracy turned into dictatorship and barbarism – or so the bourgeois myth goes. Keynesian economics offers a way out of the 1930s depression or the Long Depression now without socialism. It is the third way between the status quo of rapacious markets, austerity, inequality, poverty and crises and the alternative of social revolution that may lead to Stalin, Mao, Castro, Pol Pot and Kim Jong-Un. It is such an attractive 'third way' that Mann professes that it even appeals to him as an alternative to the risk that revolution will go wrong (see his last chapter, where Marx is portrayed as the Dr Jekyll of Hope and Keynes as the Mr Hyde of Fear).

As Mann puts it, Keynes reckoned that, if civilised experts (like himself) dealt with the short-run problems of economic crisis and slump, then the long-run disaster of the loss of civilisation could be avoided. The famous quote that makes the title of Mann's book, that 'in the long run we are all dead', was about the need to act on the Great Depression with government intervention and not wait for the market to right itself over time, as the neoclassical ('classical' Keynes called it) economists and politicians thought. For *"this long run is a misleading guide to current affairs. In the long run we are all dead. Economists set themselves too easy, too useless a task if in tempestuous seasons they can only tell us that when the storm is long past, the ocean is flat again"* (Keynes). You need to act on the short term problem or it will become a long-term disaster. This is the extra meaning of the long run quote: deal with depression and economic crises now or civilisation itself will come under threat from revolution in the long run.

Keynes liked to consider the role of economists as like dentists fixing a technical problem of toothache in the economy (*"If econo-mists could manage to get themselves thought of as humble, competent people on a level with dentists, that would be splendid"*). And modern Keynesians have likened their role as plumbers, fixing the leaks in the pipeline of accumulation and growth. But the real method of political economy is not that of a plumber or dentist fixing short-run problems. It is of a revolutionary social scientist (Marx), changing it for the long term. What the Marxist analysis of the capitalist mode of production reveals is that there is no 'third way' as Keynes and his followers would have it. Capitalism cannot deliver an end to inequality, poverty, war and a world of abundance for the common weal globally, and indeed avoid the catastrophe of environmental disaster, over the long run.

Like all bourgeois intellectuals, Keynes was an idealist. He knew that ideas only took hold if they conformed to the wishes of the ruling elite. As he put it, *"Individualism and laissez-faire could not, in spite of their deep roots in the political and moral philosophies of the late eighteenth and early nineteenth centuries, have secured their lasting hold over the conduct of public affairs, if it had not been for their conformity with the needs and wishes of the business world of the day... These many elements have contributed to the current intellectual bias, the mental make-up, the orthodoxy of the day."*. Yet he still really believed that a clever man like him with forceful ideas could change society even it was against the interests of those who controlled it.

The wrongness of that idea was brought home to him in his attempts to get the Roosevelt administration to adopt his ideas on ending the Great Depression and for the political elite to implement his ideas for a new world order after the world war. He wanted to set up 'civilised' insti-tutions to ensure peace and prosperity globally through international management of economies, currencies and money. But these ideas of a world order to control the excesses of unbridled laisser-faire capitalism were turned into institutions like the IMF, World Bank and the UN Council, used to promote the policies of imperialism, led by America. Instead of a world of 'civilised' leaders sorting out the problems of the world, we got a terrible eagle astride the globe, imposing its will. Material interests decide policies, not clever economists.

Indeed, Keynes, the great idealist of civilisation, turned into a pragmatist at the post-war Bretton Woods meetings, representing not the world's masses, or even a democratic world order, but the narrow national interests of British imperialism against American dominance. Keynes told the British parliament that the Bretton Woods deal was not *"an assertion of American power but a reasonable compromise between two great nations with the same goals; to restore a liberal world economy"*. Other nations were ignored, of course.

To avoid the situation where in the long run we are all dead, Keynes reckoned that you must sort out the short run. But the short run cannot be sorted to avoid the long run. Deliver full employment and all will be well, he thought. Yet, now, we have near 'full employment' in the US, the UK, Germany and Japan and all is not well. Real wages are stagnating, productivity is not rising and inequalities are worsening. There is a Long Depression now and no end to apparent 'secular stagnation'. Of course, the Keynesians says that this is because Keynesian policies have not been implemented. But they have not (at least not fiscal spending) because ideas do not triumph over dominant material interests, contrary to Keynes. Keynes had it upside down; in the same way that Hegel had it upside down. Hegel reckoned that it was the conflict of ideas that led to conflict in history, when it was the opposite. History is the history of class struggle.

And anyway, Keynes' economic prescriptions are based on fallacy. The long depression continues not because there is too much capital keeping down the return ('marginal efficiency') of capital relative to the rate of interest on money. There is not too much investment (business investment rates are low) and interest rates are near zero or even negative. The long depression is the result of too low profitability and so not enough investment, thus keeping down productivity growth. Low real wages and low productivity are the cost of 'full employment', contrary to all the ideas of Keynesian economics. Too much investment has not caused low profitability, but low profitability has caused too little investment.

What Mann argues is that Keynesian economics dominates the left despite its fallacies and failures because it expresses the fear that many of the leaders of the labour movement have about the masses and revolution. In other words, if we cannot manage capitalism, things could be even worse. Behind the fear of revolution is the bourgeois prejudice that to give power to 'the masses' means the end of culture, scientific progress and civilised behaviour. Yet it was the struggle of working people over the last 200 years (and before) that got all those gains of civilisation that the bourgeois is so proud of. Despite Robespierre and the revolution's 'devouring of its own children' (a term used by pro-aristocrat Mallet du Pan and adopted by the British conservative bourgeois, Edmund Burke), the French revolution opened up the expansion of science, technology in Europe. It ended feudalism, religious superstition and inquisition and introduced Napoleonic laws. If it had not taken place, France would have suffered more generations of feudal profligacy and decline.

As it is just over 100 years since the Russian revolution, we can consider the counterfactual. If the Russian revolution had not taken place, then Russian capitalism may have industrialised a little, but would have become a client state of British, French and German capital and many millions more would have been killed in a pointless and disastrous world war that Russia would have continued to participate in. Education of the masses and the development of science and technology would have been held back; as they were in China, which remained in the grip of imperialism for another generation or more. If the Chinese revolution had not taken place in 1949, China would have remained a client comprador 'failed state', controlled by Japan and the imperialist powers and ravaged by Chinese war lords, with extreme poverty and backwardness.

Keynes was a bourgeois intellectual par excellence. His advocacy of 'civilisation' meant bourgeois society to him. Indeed, economically, in his later years, he praised the very laisser-faire 'liberal' capitalism that his followers condemn now. In 1944, he wrote to Friedrich Hayek, the leading 'neo-liberal' of his time and ideological mentor of Thatcherism, in praise of his book, The Road to Serfdom, which argues that economic planning inevitably leads to totalitarianism: "*morally and philosophically I find myself in agreement with virtually the whole of it; and not only in agreement with it, but in a deeply moved agreement.*" And Keynes wrote in his very last published article, "*I find myself moved, not for the first time, to remind contemporary economists that the classical teaching embodied some permanent truths of great significance... There are in these matters deep undercurrents at work, natural forces, one can call them or even the invisible hand, which are operating towards equilibrium. If it were not so, we could not have got on even so well as we have for many decades past."*

Thus classical economics and a flat ocean returns. Once the storm (of slump and depression) has passed and the ocean is flat again, bourgeois society can breathe a sigh of relief. Keynes the radical turned into Keynes the conservative after the end of Great Depression. Will the Keynesian radicals become mainstream conservatives when the Long Depression ends?

CHAPTER 5
Marx's predictions

Inequality is inherent in capitalism

Marx predicted that inequality of wealth and incomes would tend to widen as capitalism spread its wings across the globe. There would be a concentration and centralisation of wealth in the hands of few on the one hand; and the 'immiseration' of the working class (poverty and increased exploitation) on the other. This prediction was part of Marx's law of accumulation (see chapter 2). Was he right?

A new index of human development (HDI) has been created. The origins of the HDI are found in the annual Development Reports of the United Nations Development Programme (UNDP). These had the explicit purpose *"to shift the focus of development economics from national income accounting to people-centered policies"*.

Human well-being is widely viewed as a multidimensional phenomenon of which income is only one facet. Human development defined as *"a process of enlarging people's choices"*, namely, enjoying a healthy life, acquiring knowledge and achieving a decent standard of living provides a long-run view of human well-being. The index covers up to 157 countries from the mid-19[th]century – before large-scale improvements in health helped by the diffusion of the germ theory of disease and in primary education began – to 2007, the eve of the Great Recession.

Social dimensions have driven human development gains across the board over the long run. Longevity accounts for the larger share during the first half of the 20th century. Persistent gains in lower mortality and higher survival were achieved as infectious disease gave way to chronic disease, which was experienced in developing regions from 1920 to the 1960s.

Medical technological change – including the diffusion of the germ theory of disease (1880s), new vaccines (1890s), sulpha drugs to cure infectious diseases (late 1930s) and antibiotics (1950s) – has been a main force behind the major advancement in longevity and quality of life. Economic growth also contributed to expanding longevity through nutrition improvements that strengthened the immune system and reduced morbidity and public provision of health.

What the index reveals is that there were substantial gains in world human development from the mid-19th century as the world economy industrialised and urbanised, but especially over the period 1913-1970. The major advance in human development across the board took place between 1920 and 1950, which resulted from substantial gains in longevity and education.

According to the index, although the gap between the advanced capitalist economies and the 'Third World' widened in absolute terms; in relative terms, there was a narrowing. The Russian revolution from the 1920s and the Chinese one after 1947 led to fast industrialisation and a sharp improvement in health and education for hundreds of millions. The second world war killed and displaced millions, but it also laid the basis for state intervention and the welfare state that had to be accepted by capital after the war, during the so-called 'Golden Age'.

But after 1970, the gap in human development widened once again with globalisation, rising inequalities and the capitalist neo-liberal counter-revolution. Only China closed the gap. Since 1970, longevity gains have slowed down in most emerging economies, except China, and all the world regions have fallen behind in terms of the longevity index.

What is significant is the parallel connection between economic growth, narrowing inequality and human development between 1920-1970 and the reversal of those trends since 1970. Branco Milanovic has done major work on measuring inequality of income per head between countries and regions[149] (rather than inequality within an economy). He confirms the results of the human development index. He finds that in the 1970s and 1980s, inequality between countries did not worsen.

It was the benign view of mainstream economists of the 1960s, Simon Kuznets[150] that when capitalist economies 'take off' and industrialise, inequality of incomes will rise, but eventually, as economies 'mature', income inequality declines. Thus we get a 'bell curve' of inequality and human welfare.

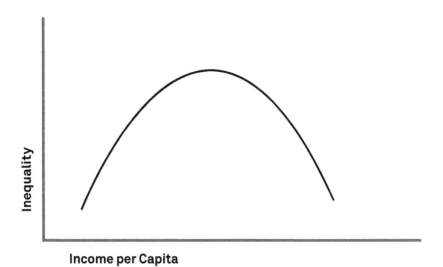

Income per Capita

But the evidence of modern capitalism in the last 40 years is the opposite. In the past 25 years, Milanovic finds what he calls 'twin peaks', rapid growth in middle-income countries, fast growth in top income countries and a slipping behind in low-income countries. Some claim that this means inequality is narrowing for all. But the falling inequality between nations that Milanovic finds (and now lauded by various right-wing economists and even some Keynesians) is almost entirely due to the stupendous growth of China which has taken hundreds of millions out of poverty.[151]

China has raised 620 million people out of internationally defined poverty. Its rate of economic growth may have been matched by emerging capitalist economies for a while back in the 19th century when they were 'taking off'. But no country has ever grown so fast and been so large (with 22% of the world's population) – only India, with 16%, is close. In 2010, 87 countries had a higher per capita GDP than China, but 83 were lower. Back in the early 1980s, three-quarters of the world's people were better off than the average Chinese. Now only 31% are. This is an achievement without precedent. Take out China and inequality between the top income countries and others has widened.

Rising inequality between countries and a worsening human development index all kicked in from the 1990s onwards as capital spread its tentacles into emerging economies (globalisation) and public sector spending on health prevention and care and on education was cut back (neoliberalism); all to reverse the low levels of profitability for capital reached globally in the early 1980s.

This connection between growth, human development and inequality between countries is also confirmed by the change in inequality of wealth and income within most economies after 1970 that Thomas Piketty and others have recorded and tried to explain. Piketty argued that there is an inherent tendency for inequality of wealth to worsen as capitalism expands: Piketty's now famous formula that r (the rate of profit for capital) will outstrip g (the rate of growth in output). But sometimes, this tendency is overcome by counter-tendencies as between 1913-1950, when g rose faster than r and inequality fell. The idea of an inherent tendency with counter-tendencies smacks of the dialectical method of analysis that Marx adopted for his own laws of motion of capitalism. Piketty misunderstood or dismissed Marx's laws and provided his own, but at least he recognised the method – now trashed by some of our modern Marxian economists.

What Piketty finds is the opposite of Kuznets' bell curve – a U-shape as the decline in inequality of wealth for the brief inter-war and early post-war period gives way to a degree of inequality not seen since the late 19th century – and according to the human development index, the end of catching up of most of the world in health, longevity and education.

Economic growth, higher incomes and wealth, development in health and education: all are key to human 'progress'. The evidence shows that in the last 30 years or so, progress has slowed significantly and the gap between the very top (whether measured by country or top 1% within a country) and the rest has widened, not narrowed.

Milanovic, Piketty and Marx have refuted the predictions of Kuznets and the apologists of capital and confirmed that of Marx.

Imperialism is a product of capitalism
At a time, in the 1840s, when capitalism was only dominant in Britain, Marx predicted that capitalism would sweep across the globe. And in

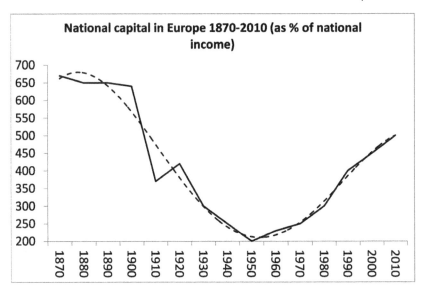

later years, Marx saw that the characteristics of modern imperialism would be found in modern capitalism. The key connection between imperialism and capitalism is the general tendency of the profitability of capital to fall over time, leading to a shifting of capital 'abroad' by national capitals seeking to reverse any fall.

When 150 years ago Marx outlined the law of tendency of the rate of profit to fall in capitalist accumulation, he made it clear that there were 'counteracting' factors to the operation of that law[152]. Indeed, this is why the law was a 'tendency' that was not always realized. One important counteracting factor was foreign trade and investment overseas. This could cheapen the cost of raw materials extracted from the colonies and could raise the rate of exploitation of the labour force by using the plentiful supplies of cheap labour (an untapped 'reserve army') in the colonial territories. The profit created by that labour could be transferred to the imperialist economies and thus raise the rate of profit at the centre.

Lenin, in his book, Imperialism[153] explained this counteracting factor as follows. *"The need to export capital arises from the fact that in a few countries capitalism has become 'overripe' and (owing to the backward state of agriculture and the poverty of the masses)"* and *"capital cannot find a field for 'profitable' investment."* This was a limited explanation. Henryk Grossman took it further[154]: *"Why,"* then, *"are profitable investments not to be found at home? The fact of capital export is as old as modern capitalism itself. The scientific task consists in explaining this fact, hence in demonstrating the role it plays in the mechanism of capitalist production."*

Marx's theory argues that there will be a tendency to equalise the rate of profit between capitals (even under monopoly capital) – indeed, this is how the higher rates of exploitation in the poor or colonial South end up in the profit rates of the rich and imperialist North. There is a transfer of value from less productive capitals of the South to more productive ones of the North.

See this example below. In both the North and the South, the rate of exploitation (s/v) in value terms is the same = 100%. The capitalists of the North use the latest technology so that the time taken to produce the value of labour power is much less (20v) than in the South where the capitalists use less technology and more cheap labour. But the rate of exploitation is the same in this example (North 20/20 and South 60/60).

North: 80c + 20v + 20s=120V. Rate of profit = 20/(80c+20v) = 20% Rate of exploitation = 20s/20v = 100%

South: 40c + 60v + 60s= 160V. Rate of profit = 60/(40c+60v) = 60% Rate of exploitation = 60s/60v = 100%

Total: 120c + 80v + 80s= 280V. Average rate of profit = 80s/(120c+80v) = 40%.

The capitalists in the South get 160V in value out of their workers, while the capitalists in the North get less, 120V. The rate of profit in value terms in the North would only be 20% while it would be 60% in the South. But competition in the global market equalizes the average rate of profit at 40%. So the market price of production for the North and South is 140 and the North gets a transfer of value of 20 from the South – an unequal exchange. The capitalists of the North get some of the value created by the workers in the South through price competition equalizing the rate of profit on the global market.

North = 80c + 20v + 40s = 140P (compared to 120V), so transfer gain of 20.

South = 40c + 60v + 40s = 140P (compared to 160V), so transfer loss of 20.

Now suppose that the workers in the South are 'super-exploited' and forced to accept a lower wage (halved from 60v to 30v in the above example). Now the surplus value in the South is way higher (and the rate of surplus value is now 300% compared to 100% in the North). The process of the global market produces an average rate of profit that is higher than before, at 65%.

North = 80c + 20v + 20s = 120V. Rate of profit 20s/(80c+20v) = 20%. Rate of exploitation 20s/20v = 100%

South = 40c + 30v + 90s = 160V. Rate of profit 90s/(40c+30v) = 130%. Rate of exploitation 90s/30v = 300%

Total = 120c + 50v + 110s = 280V. Average rate of profit 110s/(120c+50v) = 65%

Through the transfer of values in the global market, the capitalists of the North now get an extra 45V out of the super-exploited workers of the South. Super-exploitation in the South increases profits for the North. Total surplus value in the North and South has risen from 80 in the first case to 110 in the super-exploitation case.

North = 80c + 20v + 65s = 165P (compared to 120V), so transfer gain of 45.

South = 40c + 30v + 45s = 115P (compared to 160V), so transfer loss of 45.

The wages of the workers of the North are unchanged. In this sense, the workers of the North are not 'living off' those of the South. Both the capitalists of the South and the North are exploiting the workers of the South by squeezing more value out of them.

It is the race for higher rates of profit that is the motive power of world capitalism and the driver of imperialism and rivalry among imperialist nation-states. Foreign trade can yield a surplus profit for the advanced country. From about the mid-1960s onwards, the rate of profit fell in the major economies to reach a post-war low by the early 1980s.

So the leading capitalist states again looked to counteract Marx's law through renewed capital flows into countries that had massive potential reserves of labour that would be submissive and accept 'super-exploiting' wages. World trade barriers were lowered, restrictions on cross-border capital flows were reduced and multi-national corporations moved capital at will within their corporate accounts. This explains the policies of the major imperialist states at home (an intensified attack on the working class) and abroad (a drive to transform foreign nations into tributaries). Globalisation is thus a product of the drive to raise profitability after its significant decline in the major capitalist economies from the mid-1960s to the early 1980s.

This connection between the changes in the rate of profit in the major capitalist economies and globalization from the 1980s can be shown to have a common thread ever since capitalism became the dominant mode of production in the world, starting with Europe, the US and Japan in the mid-19th century. Moreover, it appears that in a particularly long period of low profitability and stagnation in production,

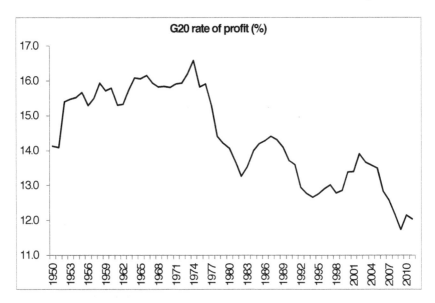

imperialist rivalry in the struggle of the share of global surplus value becomes intense. Competition among imperialist powers for the spoils of exploitation turns into capturing the spoils of war.

There have been three depressions in the history of capitalism: one in the late 19th century; the Great Depression of the 1930s; and the current Long Depression[155]. They coincided with different stages of capitalism. The depression of the late 19th century was the impulse for the development of modern imperialism, namely the expansion of finance capital into the "colonies" and the battle among imperialist powers to divide up the world, which eventually led to World War I.

The Great Depression of the late 19th century led to a new imperialist battle, one that was not resolved by World War I. The hegemonic imperialist power, Great Britain, had been irretrievably weakened by the 1914–18 war, but the rising hegemonic power, the United States, was not ready or willing to assume the mantle of imperialist dominance. The rising imperialist powers, Germany and Japan, tried to gain a bigger cut of the spoils. That led to World War II and the eventual assumption of Pax Americana after 1945. The current Long Depression could also give way to a new period of imperialist rivalry.

Globalisation of trade and capital took off whenever profitability of capital fell in the imperialist centres. Between 1832-48, profitability of capital in the major economies fell; after which there was an expansion of globalization to drive up profitability (1850-70). However, a new fall in profitability led to the first depression of the late 19th century (1870-90), during which protectionism rose and capital flows shrunk. With economic recovery after 1890, imperialist rivalry intensified, leading up to the Great War of 1914-18.

In the post-1918 period, after the defeats of various European revolutions and the isolation of the Soviet state, there was a brief period of rising profitability, before a new drop led into the Great Depression of the 1930s. Imperialist rivalry bubbled up again, leading to WW2.

Again after the defeats of various labour struggles post 1945 in Europe, Japan and in the colonial territories, capitalism entered a new 'golden age' of relatively fast growth and rising profitability. Globalisation of trade (reduction in tariffs and protectionism) and capital (dollar-led economies and international institutions) revived, until profitability again began to fall in the 1970s. The 1970s saw a weakening of trade liberalization and capital flows. From the 1980s, however, capitalism saw a new expansion of globalization in trade and capital to restore profitability.

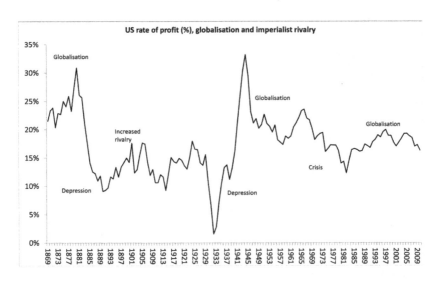

We can divide globalization into three great waves[156]. The first wave was from 1860-1914 when Europe and North America were strongly affected by internationalisation. The flow of goods accelerated. Capital moved relatively freely between countries. In some respects financial integration was more pronounced than it is today. Even international migration was greater than it is today. Roughly 60 million people left Europe to seek their fortunes in the New World. Great Britain was the world's leading economy.

The basis for the European free trade system was the 1860 free trade pact between Great Britain and France, just as Marx was writing Capital. Many other European countries subsequently aligned themselves with this free trade system. However, from the 1870s, in the depression period, a Russian and American 'grain invasion' prompted higher tariffs in most of continental Europe. So overall trade costs did not decline dramatically after 1870 since tariffs and non-tariff barriers rose

In the second wave after WW2, international regulations and organisations to support economic integration at the global level were created. Cooperation was based on the Bretton Woods Agreement of 1944. The USA was now the leading economy in the world and the dollar became the monetary basis of the financial system. The 'Bretton Woods system' meant that nations had fixed currency exchanges in relation to the US dollar, which in turn was fixed to the gold standard.

Two organisations were established during this period, the World Bank (IBRD) and the International Monetary Fund (IMF). In addition a special agreement, the General Agreement on Tariffs and Trade (GATT) became operative in 1948. In practice GATT became the international organisation which set the framework for several important steps towards increased global free trade, particularly via successive reductions in industrial tariffs. But by 1970 the Bretton Woods system was coming under increasing pressure.

In the third wave from the mid-1980s, the more populous countries in the developing world, particularly China and India, have opened their doors to the world. European cooperation has widened and deepened. In the decades up to the end of 20th century, international trade grew significantly faster than total production. The export of goods amounted to 31% of global GDP in 2006 as compared to 12% in 1970. Foreign direct investment (establishing or buying up companies abroad) has increased twice as fast as trade. An even more rapid increase has been seen in foreign securities (investments that do not lead to controlled ownership in foreign companies).

This third wave is visible in the expansion of gross foreign assets (capital invested abroad) since the 1980s. The ratio of global foreign assets to global GDP more than doubled – from 7% in 1870 to 19% in 1900. This upswing was reversed during the first half of the 20th century. The mayhem created by two world wars and the Great Depression on the one hand and the emergence of domestic 'institutionalized waste' on the other undermined the flow of capital and caused the share of foreign ownership to recede. But by 2003, after a quarter century of exponential growth, it reached an all-time high of 122%.

According to the McKinsey Global Institute[157], between 1990 and 2006 the global proportion of foreign-owned assets has nearly tripled, from 9% to 26% of all world assets (both foreign and domestically-owned). The increase was broadly based: foreign ownership of corporate bonds rose from 7% to 21% of the world total, foreign ownership of government bonds rose from 11% to 31% and foreign ownership of corporate stocks rose from 9% to 27%.

As we reach the 200th anniversary of Marx's birth, capitalism has become truly global. That's because increased investment into emerging capitalist economies brought into the capitalist mode of production a huge supply of peasant and non-capitalist labour and much of it at a cost below poverty levels - what Marx called 'super-exploitation'.

At the same time, imperialist economies are acting even more as bases for finance capital globally. US corporation revenues from abroad are worth $3bn a day and total more than the annual GDP of Switzerland. A financial company operating in a major international financial centre can draw upon the surplus value produced anywhere in the world, for the ultimate benefit of the imperialist power in which it is based. Just 147 companies globally control the world.[158]

However, the world of international business is still a regional one, not a global one. Capitalism today remains divided, whatever the degree of its global integration, into distinct capitalist nation-states, ruled by their own capitalist classes, which project their interests and protect those interests against rivals. In 1980, when US 'financialization' started in earnest, US owners accounted for only 28% of global foreign assets. But by 2003, the asset share of US owners was reduced to a mere 18%.

In the previous wave of globalisation after 1950, power shifted from owners in one core country (Britain) to those in another (the United States). By contrast, in the next wave, the contenders could be from China, OPEC, Russia, Brazil, Korea and India, among others. They have become major foreign investors with significant international assets, including large stakes in America's 'imperial' debt.

The beginning of the 21st century brought to an end the third wave of globalisation. Profitability in the major imperialist economies peaked by the early 2000s and after the short credit-fuelled burst of up to 2007, they entered the Great Recession, which was followed a by a new long depression. Like that of the late 19the century, this brought to an end this globalisation. World trade growth is now no faster than world output growth, or even slower. So the counteracting factor to low profitability of exports of commodities and credit has died away. This threatens the hegemony of US imperialism, already in relative decline to new ambitious powers like China, Brazil, India and Russia. Renewed rivalry threatens to unleash major conflicts in the next decade or so.

World trade growth in 2016 was well below the post-Great Recession average of 2.7% a year, which in turn is less than half the rate of world trade growth before the global financial crash (at 5.7%).[159] As the IMF put it: *"Since 2012, growth in the volume of world trade in goods and services has been less than half the rate during the preceding three decades. It has barely kept pace with world GDP and the slowdown has been widespread.*[160]

McKinsey outlined why global trade and industrial growth has slowed to a crawl since the end of the Great Recession in 2009[161]. *"The shock of the 2008 global financial crisis triggered the first recorded drop in global*

GDP and the hangover has since persisted, with many countries struggling with unexpectedly weak recoveries." And it is not going to get any better. *"More worryingly, long-term growth prospects are serious cause for concern. Annual GDP growth from 2014 to 2064 is projected to effectively halve, falling to 2.1% globally and 1.9% for developed countries".*

Deutsche Bank economists recently concluded that *"It feels like we're coming towards the end of an economic era. Such eras often come and go in long waves. In the past 30 years a perfect storm of factors — China re-entering the global economy in the 70s, the fall of the Soviet Union, and to some extent, the economic liberalisation of India — added more than a billion workers into the global labour market."* [162]

Globalization and the high-tech revolution reversed the productivity growth decline in the 1990s. But in this century productivity growth in the advanced economies has headed toward stagnation. Only productivity growth in the emerging economies has enabled world productivity growth to stay near 2% a year. Since the Great Recession, productivity growth has dropped to under 1% a year.

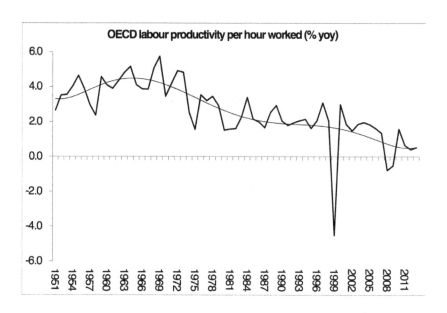

OECD labour productivity per hour worked (% yoy)

What the productivity growth figures show is that the ability of capitalism (or at least the advanced capitalist economies) to generate better productivity is receding. Capitalists have squeezed the share of new value going to labour and raised the profit share to compensate. Above all, they have cut back on the rate of capital accumulation in the 'real economy', increasingly trying to find extra profit in financial and property speculation.

The story on productivity is repeated for employment growth in the advanced economies. Employment growth is far less than 1% a year in the 21st century. If you add (to productivity growth) an employment growth rate globally of 1% a year, then global growth is going to be little more than 3% a year for the next decade (and a maximum of just 2% a year for the advanced economies). The dynamism of world capitalism is waning.

Some argue that after its 60-year decline, manufacturing may start to return to the advanced capitalist economies. Then profitability will rise again in the major capitalist economies through a new manufacturing revolution. This is the theme of US President Trump, who reckons he can cajole American manufacturers to produce at home and restrict cheap imports from China etc.

But this is really just so much wishful thinking. American manufacturing has been growing in the past few years, but the sector still has 2 million fewer jobs than when the Great Recession began. Worldwide manufacturing is growing much faster, even for many of the American-owned companies that are expanding at home. Wage levels may have risen in emerging economies and stagnated in the advanced economies, but the gap is still huge. Hourly compensation costs for manufacturing in the US were about four times those in Taiwan and 20 times those in the Philippines.

As John Smith has shown[163]: *"about 80% of global trade (in terms of gross exports) is linked to the international production networks of transnational corporations"*. UNCTAD estimates that *"about 60% of global trade ... consists of trade in intermediate goods and services that are incorporated at various stages in the production process of goods and services for final consumption"*. A striking feature of contemporary globalisation is that a very large and growing proportion of the workforce in many global value chains is now located in developing economies. In a phrase, the centre of gravity of much of the world's industrial production has *"shifted from the north to the south of the global economy"*. Reversing this key feature of what has been called 'globalisation' can only be damaging to American corporations, while at the same time shifting the burden of any cost and prices rises onto average American households.

On a standard measure of participation in global value chains produced by the IMF, the rise in profitability for the major multinationals is now stalling. Sure, information flows (internet traffic and telephone calls, mainly) have exploded, but trade and capital flows are still below their pre-recession peaks. Global foreign direct investment as a share of GDP is also falling and capital flows to the so-called 'emerging economies' have plummeted.

Some strategists of capital are worried that Trumponomics will only make things worse for profitability globally. Lorenzo Bini Smaghi, ex-member of the European Central Bank's executive board and a leading strategist of finance capital, commented: *"Trying to reverse globalisation can be damaging, particularly for the country that takes the first step. It is the advanced economies that are facing the greatest challenges in its most recent wave, which is why anti-globalisation movements are gaining support and governments are tempted to become inward-looking. However, because their economies are so large, and so bound by the web of globalisation, they cannot reverse its course, unless emerging markets also retreat"*.[164]

The world economy is in a Long Depression. However, world capitalism will not stay in this depressed state. Eventually, probably after another slump that will destroy sufficient value (the value of means of production, fictitious capital and employment), profitability for those capitals that survive will rise again to start an new upwave in investment and growth. This assumes, of course, that the class struggle does not lead to the forces of labour triumphing over capital in any major imperialist economy.

A new wave of globalization is thus possible. There are yet more human beings in the world to be exploited and there are always new technological innovations that can provide a new cycle for expansion of value and surplus value. There are still huge reserves of labour as yet untapped, particularly in Africa. The latest UN projections for the world's economies show that Africa is expected to dominate population growth over the next ninety years as populations in many of the world's developed economies and China shrink.[165] Africa's population is expected to more than quadruple over just 90 years, while Asia will continue to grow but peak about 50 years from now and then start declining.

Can capitalism get a further kick forward from exploiting these hundreds of millions coming into the labour forces of Asia, South America, and the Middle East? While the industrial workforce in the mature capitalist economies has shrunk to under 150 million; in the so-called emerging economies the industrial workforce now stands at 500 million, having surpassed the industrial workforce in the imperialist countries by the early 1980s. In addition, there is a large reserve army of labour composed of unemployed, underemployed, or inactive adults of another 2.3 billion people that could also be exploited for new value.

But competition and imperialist rivalry will grow, just as Marx and Lenin predicted. America's intelligence services also looked recently at developments in the world economy. The Office of the Director of National Intelligence (DNI) published its latest assessment, called <u>Global Trends: The Paradox of Progress</u>,[166] which *"explores trends and scenarios*

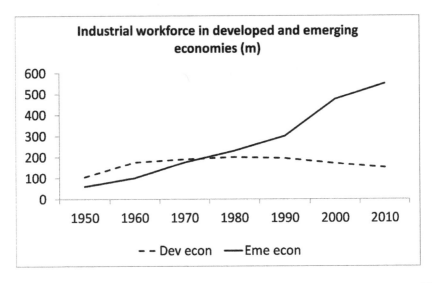

over the next 20 years". And the DNI reckons that things are not going to get better: *"The next five years will see rising tensions within and between countries. Global growth will slow, just as increasingly complex global challenges impend."*

What is the answer? Well, this comment from the DNI report is unvarnished: *"It will be tempting to impose order on this apparent chaos, but that ultimately would be too costly in the short run and would fail in the long. Dominating empowered, proliferating actors in multiple domains would require unacceptable resources in an era of slow growth, fiscal limits, and debt burdens. Doing so domestically would be the end of democracy, resulting in authoritarianism or instability or both. Although material strength will remain essential to geopolitical and state power, the most powerful actors of the future will draw on networks, relationships, and information to compete and cooperate. This is the lesson of great power politics in the 1900s, even if those powers had to learn and relearn it."* In other words, while it would be better to just crush opposition and *"impose order"* in America's interests, this is probably not possible with a weak world economy and lack of funds. Better to try *"draw on networks, relationships and information"* (ie spy and manipulate) to get *"cooperation".*

But it is not going to be easy to sustain America's dominance and the rule of capital, the DNI report concludes, as globalisation has *"hollowed out Western middle classes* (read working classes) *and stoked a pushback against globalization."* Moreover, *"migrant flows are greater now than in the past 70 years, raising the specter of drained welfare coffers and increased competition for jobs, and reinforcing nativist, anti-elite impulses."* And *"slow growth plus technology-induced disruptions in job markets will threaten poverty reduction and drive tensions within countries in the years to come, fueling the very nationalism that contributes to tensions between countries."*

Imperialism has two Achilles heels. The first is the tendency of the rate of profit to fall as capitalism accumulates, posing increased rivalry and even damaging and destructive wars. The second is the global proletariat – the gravediggers of capitalism – who are still growing in size across the world. The global proletariat has never been larger in the history of capitalism. In that sense, Marx's prophecy in the Communist Manifesto

170 years ago is confirmed. Sure, the majority of the proletariat is now in the South and not the North. But that does not mean the workers of the North will play no role in ending capitalism. On the contrary, they are the key to ending imperialism in its centre.

Capitalism will destroy the planet

The environmental and ecological impact of the capitalist mode of production was highlighted by Marx and Engels way back in the early part of industrialisation in Europe. As Engels put it, capitalism is production for profit and not human need and so takes no account of the impact on wider society of accumulation for profit: *"As individual capitalists are engaged in production and exchange for the sake of the immediate profit, only the nearest, most immediate results must first be taken into account. As long as the individual manufacturer or merchant sells a manufactured or purchased commodity with the usual coveted profit, he is satisfied and does not concern himself with what afterwards becomes of the commodity and its purchasers."* This drive for profit leads to ecological catastrophe: *"What cared the Spanish planters in Cuba, who burned down forests on the slopes of the mountains and obtained from the ashes sufficient fertilizer for one generation of very highly profitable coffee trees–what cared they that the heavy tropical rainfall afterwards washed away the unprotected upper stratum of the soil, leaving behind only bare rock!"*[167]

Marx summed up the impact of capitalist production on nature: *"All progress in capitalistic agriculture is a progress in the art, not only of robbing the labourer, but of robbing the soil; all progress in increasing the fertility of the soil for a given time, is a progress towards ruining the lasting sources of that fertility...Capitalist production, therefore, develops technology, and the combining together of various processes into a social whole, only by sapping the original sources of all wealth–the soil and the labourer."*

And there is now overwhelming evidence that climate change and global warming is the result of capitalist accumulation. Jose Tapia and Oscar Carpintero[168] have shown that there is a pro-cyclical correlation between the rate of increase of atmospheric CO_2 and the rate of growth of the global economy, providing strong evidence that the world economy is linked with the build-up of the greenhouse effect and, therefore, with the process of global warming. In another paper, Tapia uses multivariate analysis of the influence of the world economy, volcanic activity and ENSO activity on CO_2 levels to show that the annual increase in atmospheric CO_2 is significantly linked to the growth of the global economy. Years of above-trend GDP growth are years of greater rise in CO_2 concentrations, and similarly, years of below-trend growth are years of smaller rise in CO_2 concentrations. So global emissions of CO_2 have increased at rates strongly correlated with the absolute growth of the global economy.

This might well provide part of the explanation of the slowdown in global warming from 1998, as world economic growth slowed since then. A major drop in the growth of estimated emissions occurred in 2009 as a consequence of the Great Recession. When capitalist production stops, so does global warming. Of course, that does not end the story. As Tapia goes onto to say: *"However, even in 2009 when the global economy contracted 2.25%, global emissions did not decrease, they just ceased growing to start growing again next year when the world economy somewhat recovered. This shows how dependent on fossil fuels the world economy has become in recent years. In earlier recessions of the global economy — in the mid-1970s, early-1980s, early-1990s and late-1990s— emissions not only decreased in many countries, as we have shown, but also worldwide. The notion that economic growth will reduce the carbon intensity of the world economy (the ratio of global emissions to WGDP) is inconsistent with the fact that the carbon intensity of the global economy has increased in recent years. In 2010, after the Great Recession, WGDP grew 5.0%, but emissions grew faster, 5.9%. Furthermore, the average growth of global CO_2 emissions was 3.1% per year in 2000-2011, while it had been 1.0% per year in 1990–2000, and 2.0% per year in 1980-1990".*

Most of the rise in emissions comes from emerging economies where economic growth has been fastest. China was responsible for 24 per cent of the global total emissions in 2009, against 17 per cent for the US and 8 per cent for the eurozone. But each Chinese person emits only a third as much as an American and less than four-fifths of a resident of the eurozone. China is a relatively wasteful emerging economy, in terms of its emissions per unit of output. But it still emits less per head than the high-income countries because its people remain relatively poor. As emerging countries develop, emissions per person will tend to rise towards levels in high-income countries, raising the global average. This is why global emissions per person rose by 16 per cent between 2000 and 2009, which was a period of fast growth in emerging economies.

What could solve this disaster? Maybe new technology like carbon capture, transport not based on fossil fuels, produced locally with low carbon footprints etc – and, of course, a shift out of fossil fuels into renewables. But it is not just a problem of carbon and other gas emissions, but of cleaning up the environment that is already damaged. All these tasks require public control and ownership of the energy and transport industries and public investment in the environment for the public good. There is no sign of that. Disasters are not only more imminent and but with us already in the form of floods, tsunamis, droughts and other 'natural' nightmares.

The inexorable rise of the machines

Over 150 years ago Marx discussed the replacement of human labour by machines: *"The real facts, which are travestied by the optimism of the economists, are these: the workers, when driven out of the workshop by the machinery, are thrown onto the labour-market. Their presence in the labour-market increases the number of labour-powers which are at the disposal of capitalist exploitation...the effect of machinery, which has been represented as a compensation for the working class, is, on the contrary, a most frightful scourge. For the present I will only say this: workers who have been thrown out of work in a given branch of industry can no doubt look for employment in another branch...even if they do find employment, what a miserable prospect they face! Crippled as they are by the division of labour, these poor devils are worth so little outside their old trade that they cannot find admission into any industries except a few inferior and therefore over-supplied and under-paid branches. Furthermore, every branch of industry attracts each year a new stream of men, who furnish a contingent from which to fill up vacancies, and to draw a supply for expansion. As soon as machinery has set free a part of the workers employed in a given branch of industry, the reserve men are also diverted into new channels of employment, and become absorbed in other branches; meanwhile the original victims, during the period transition, for the most part starve and perish."*[169]

"We have seen how this absolute contradiction (namely the contradiction

between the revolutionary technical basis of large-scale industry and the form it takes under capitalism) does away with all repose, all fixity and all security as far as the worker's life-situation is concerned; how it constantly threatens, by taking away the instruments of labour, to snatch from his hands the means of subsistence, and, by suppressing his specialised function, to make him superfluous. We have seen, too, how this contradiction bursts forth without restraint in the ceaseless human sacrifices required from the working class, in the reckless squandering of labour-powers, and in the devastating effects of social anarchy. This is the negative side."

Marx emphasized that *"the inseparable contradictions and antagonisms of the capitalist use of the machine"*. It is that *"considered in itself, the machine abbreviates the working time; while used by the capitalists, it prolongs it"*. Also *"in itself, it facilitates the work, but used by the capitalists, it increases its intensity"*. Likewise *"in itself is a victory of man over the forces of nature, but employed by the capitalists imposes on man the yoke of natural forces."* Finally, *"considered in itself increases the wealth of the producer, but when used by the capitalists, it pauperizes"* [170]

So there is a contradiction: between the content of the means of production -which leads to an increase in the production of values of use, of material wealth and its capitalist social form -that is, based on the exploitation of labour. Will this contradiction lead to the wiping out of human labour in production and with it the livelihood of billions?

Two Oxford economists, Carl Benedikt Frey and Michael Osborne,[171] looked at the likely impact of technological change on a sweeping range of 702 occupations, from podiatrists to tour guides, animal trainers to personal finance advisers and floor sanders. Their conclusions were: *"According to our estimates, about 47 percent of total US employment is at risk. We further provide evidence that wages and educational attainment exhibit a strong negative relationship with an occupation's probability of computerisation....Rather than reducing the demand for middle-income occupations, which has been the pattern over the past decades, our model predicts that computerisation will mainly substitute for low-skill and low-wage jobs in the near future. By contrast, high-skill and high-wage occupations are the least susceptible to computer capital."*

A World Economic Forum study[172] reckoned that increased automation and AI in the workforce will lead to the loss of 7.1m jobs over the next five years in 15 leading economies, while helping create just 2m new jobs over the same period. In the financial sector, a thinking, learning and trading computer may well make even today's superfast, ultra-complex investment algorithms look archaic — and possibly render human fund managers redundant. You might say we don't care too much about losing hedge fund managers. But AI and robots will destroy the jobs of millions in productive sectors and create jobs on much less money.

In contrast, there was a study by economists at the consultancy Deloitte on the relationship between jobs and the rise of technology by trawling through census data for England and Wales going back to 1871. Their conclusion is unremittingly cheerful[173]. Rather than destroying jobs, technology historically has been a *"great job-creating machine"*. Findings by Deloitte such as a four-fold rise in bar staff since the 1950s or a surge in the number of hairdressers this century suggest to the authors that technology has increased spending power, therefore creating new demand and new jobs. *"The dominant trend is of contracting employment in agriculture and manufacturing being more than offset by rapid growth in the caring, creative, technology and business services sectors,"* they write. *"Machines will take on more repetitive and labourious tasks, but seem no closer to eliminating the need for human labour than at any time in the last 150 years."*

Technology can lead to workers being displaced in one particular industry, but this doesn't hold for the economy as a whole. In Paul Krugman's celebrated example[174], imagine there are two goods, sausages and bread rolls, which are then combined one for one to make hot dogs. 120 million workers are divided equally between the two industries: 60 million producing sausages, the other 60 million producing rolls, and both taking two days to produce one unit of output.

Now suppose technology doubles productivity in bakeries. Fewer workers are required to make rolls, but this increased productivity will mean that consumers get 33% more hot dogs. Eventually the economy has 40 million workers making rolls, and 80 million making sausages. In the interim, the transition might lead to unemployment, particularly if skills are very specific to the baking industry. But in the long run, a change in relative productivity reallocates rather than destroys employment.

The story of bank tellers vs the cash machine (ATM) is a great example of a technological innovation entirely replacing human labour for a particular task. Did this led to a massive fall in the number of bank tellers? Between the 1970s (when American's first ATM was installed) and 2010, the number of bank tellers doubled. As James Bessen notes, reducing the number of tellers per branch made it cheaper to run a branch, so banks expanded their branch networks. And the role gradually evolved away from cash handling and more towards relationship banking.

So if many of today's jobs can be entirely replaced by machines, technology can also create new roles. At the end of the 19th century, half the US workforce was employed in agriculture, and this employment was rendered obsolete by technical change. But in that time a whole raft of new occupations – electrical engineer, computer programmer, etc – have been created.

Also, previous economy-wide transformational changes don't happen in a short space of time. The industrial revolution, although drastic in the broader sweep of human history, took at least 50 years. If an underlying innovation occurs in a single "big bang" like the railways, or electricity, it can take time for the implications to fan out to the wider economy, even if particular industries are affected much quicker. So which way will it be?

Will the information revolution reduce working time under capitalism and thus lead progressively to post-capitalism? In recent work, Graetz and Michaels[175] looked at 14 industries (mainly manufacturing industries, but also agriculture and utilities) in 17 developed countries (including European countries, Australia, South Korea, and the US) They found that industrial robots had no significant effect on total hours worked. But they did lead to a loss of jobs for the unskilled and even those with some skills.

As productivity rises, people could just work fewer hours and enjoy the same level of consumption. But equally, they could work the same hours and devote the productivity boost entirely to raising consumption or, more likely, enjoy a bit more of both. This so-called "income effect" means working hours should fall, but by less than one for one with the rise in productivity.

But that's not the only thing going on – rising productivity tilts the relative prices of leisure and consumption in favour of the latter – what economists call the "substitution effect". Gregory Clarke suggests that in 1700 a craftsman needed to work for almost 10 hours to earn the 2 old pence required to purchase a kilo of beef. But by 2014, a median UK worker can earn the ten pounds or so need to buy that kilo of beef in less than hour. And so measured in beef, or goods in general, the reward for working that extra hour is much bigger.[176]

The overall effect on hours depends on the balance of the two. Angus Maddison's 2001 *magnum opus* estimates that between 1820 and 1998, real GDP per capita in Western Europe increased 15-fold.[177] Over the same period hours declined by about a half. So the productivity dividend was split about 7:1 in favour of consumption. On that basis, unless automation leads to vast productivity gains, any fall in hours would be modest and slow. It would take a 75% rise in productivity to deliver a 10% fall in hours. Or a 150% rise to knock a day off the working week.

What does this all mean if we enter the extreme (science fiction?) future where robotic technology and AI leads to robots making robots AND robots extracting raw materials and making everything AND carrying out all personal and public services so that human labour is no longer required for ANY task of production at all? Let's imagine a totally auto-mated process where no human worked in the production process. Surely, value has been added by the conversion of raw materials into goods without humans? Surely, that refutes Marx's claim that only human labour can create value?

In Marx's economic theory, abstract labour is the only source of value and surplus-value. However, in the case of an economy where robots build robots build robots and there is no human labour involved, surely value is still created? This was the argument of Dmitriev in 1898, in his critique of Marx's value theory[178]. He said that, in a fully automa-ted system, a certain input of machines can create a greater output of machines (or of other commodities). In this case, profit and the rate of profit would be determined exclusively by the technology used (productivity) and not by (abstract) labour. If 10 machines produce 12 machines, the profit is 2 machines and the rate of profit is 2/10 = 20%.

Value reduced to use value has nothing to do with Marx's notion of value, which is the monetary expression of abstract labour expended by labourers. If machines could create 'value', this value would be use-value rather than value as the outcome of humans' abstract labour. But, if machines can create 'value', so can an infinity of other factors (animals, the forces of nature, sunspots, etc.) and the determination of value becomes impossible. And if machines supposedly could transfer their use-value to the product, this would immediately crash against the problem of the aggregation of different use-values.

For Marx, machines do not create value. Rather, concrete labour transfers the value of the machines (and, more generally, of the means of production) to the product. They increase human productivity and thus the output per unit of capital invested, while decreasing the quantity of living labour needed for the production of a certain output. Given that only labour creates value, the substitution of the means of production for living labour decreases the quantity of value created per unit of capital invested.

If machines as well as labour were considered to create value, the same quantity of value would be produced by a unit of capital invested, irrespective of the relative percentage-weight of machines and labour. For this approach, 90% machines and 10% labour would create just as much value as 10% machines and 90% labour (so that 90% machines would create more value than 10% machines). In Marx's theory, on the contrary, 90% machines and 10% labour create much less value than in the opposite case. It follows that, in the former case, lower profit-rates and thus crises are not originated by a decreased production of (surplus-) value due to less living labour employed, whereas for Marx this is indeed the case.

In the former approach, labour-shedding and productivity-increasing technological innovations leave the production of value unchanged, so that the greater the capital invested the greater the production of value. In the latter approach (Marx), the greater the capital invested by introducing labour-shedding and productivity-increasing means of production, the greater the fall in employment, the less the value produced and incorporated in a greater quantity of output.

In the former approach, technological innovations lead to economic growth. In the latter, they lead tendentially to crises. Given that labour-shedding and productivity-increasing technological innovations are the motor of capitalism's dynamic, for the former approach capitalism tends towards growth and reproduction while, for the latter (Marx), it tends towards crises and its own supersession.

The Dmitriev critique confuses the dual nature of value under capitalism: use value and exchange value. There is use value (things and services that people need); and exchange value (the value measured in labour time and appropriated from human labour by the owners of capital and realised by sale on the market). In every commodity under the capitalist mode of production, there is both use value and exchange value. You can't have one without the other under capitalism. But the latter rules the capitalist investment and production process, not the former.

Value (as defined) is specific to capitalism. Sure, living labour can create things and do services (use values). But value is the substance of the capitalist mode of producing things. Capital (the owners) controls the means of production created by labour and will only put them to use in order to appropriate value created by labour. Capital does not create value itself. So in our hypothetical all-encompassing robot/AI world, productivity (of use values) would tend to infinity while profitability (surplus value to capital value) would tend to zero.

The essence of capitalist accumulation is that to increase profits and accumulate more capital, capitalists want to introduce machines that can boost the productivity of each employee and reduce costs compared to competitors. This is the great revolutionary role of capitalism in developing the productive forces available to society.

But there is a contradiction. In trying to raise the productivity of labour with the introduction of technology, there is a process of labour shedding. New technology replaces labour. Yes, increased productivity might lead to increased output and open up new sectors for employment to compensate. But over time, a 'capital-bias' or labour shedding means less new value is created (as labour is the only content of value) relative to the cost of invested capital. So there is a tendency for profitability to fall as productivity rises. In turn, that leads eventually to a crisis in production that halts or even reverses the gain in production from the new technology. This is solely because investment and production depend on the profitability of capital in our modern (capitalist) mode of production.

This is no longer capitalism. The analogy is more with a slave economy as in ancient Rome. In ancient Rome, over hundreds of years, the formerly predominantly small-holding peasant economy was replaced by slaves in mining, farming and all sorts of other tasks. This happened because the booty of the successful wars that the Roman republic and empire conducted included a mass supply of slave labour. The cost to the slave owners of these slaves was incredibly cheap (to begin with) compared with employing free labour. The slave owners drove the farmers off their land through a combination of debt demands, requisition in wars and sheer violence. The former peasants and their families were forced into slavery themselves or into the cities, where they scraped a living with menial tasks and skills or begged. The class struggle did not end. The struggle was between the slave-owning aristocrats and the slaves and between the aristocrats and the atomised plebs in the cities.

A fully robot economy means that the owners of the means of production (robots) would have a super-abundant economy of things and services at zero cost (robots making robots making robots). The owners can then just consume. They don't need to make 'profit', just as the aristocrat slave owners in Rome just consumed and did not run businesses to sell commodities to make a profit. So a robotic economy could mean a super-abundant world for all or it could mean a new form of slave society with extreme inequality of wealth and income. It's a social 'choice' or more accurately, it depends of the outcome of the class struggle under capitalism.

The key issue is Marx's law of the tendency of the rate of profit to fall. A rising organic composition of capital leads to a fall in the overall rate of profit engendering recurring crises. If robots and AI do replace human labour at an accelerating rate, that can only intensify that tendency. Well before we get to a robot-all world, capitalism will experience ever-increasing periods of crises and stagnation.

Paul Mason in his book, Post capitalism[179], makes much of Marx's discussion of the role of technology in his Fragment on Machines from the Grundrisse written in 1857.[180] In Mason's interpretation, Marx reckons that capitalism expands technology and scientific knowledge to the point that a world of abundance and free time for all becomes reality. As Mason puts it: *"In an economy where machines do most of the work, the nature of the knowledge locked inside the machines must, he writes, be "social". ...it suggests that, once knowledge becomes a productive force in its own right, outweighing the actual labour spent creating a machine, the big question becomes not one of "wages versus profits" but who controls what Marx called the "power of knowledge".*

It is true that the development of the productive forces has now created the pre-conditions for a society of abundance and an end of class exploitation. It is what Engels said in 1880 when he summed up the state of capitalism and Marxism as scientific socialism as opposed to utopian socialism. *"The possibility of securing for every member of society, by means of socialized production, an existence not only fully sufficient materially, and becoming day-by-day more full, but an existence guaranteeing to all the free development and exercise of their physical and mental faculties — this possibility is now, for the first time, here"[181].*

But Mason's version is a one-sided and utopian view of technological progress. If you read the Fragment carefully, you can see that Marx is not posing some steady and harmonious development of a world of abundance through scientific knowledge embodied in an 'ideal machine'. Yes, use values will multiply through technological advance, but this creates a contradiction within capitalism that will not disappear gradually. Under capitalism, increased knowledge from science and human labour is incorporated into machines. But machines are owned by capital not society in common. The class struggle does not disappear under the 'power of knowledge'. On the contrary, it can intensify[182].

Technical advances to meet the needs of people, to help end poverty and create a society of superabundance without damaging the environment and the ecology of the planet are what we want. If AI/robotic technology can bring us closer to that, all the better. Marx:[183] *"The free development of individualities, and hence not the reduction of necessary labour time so as to posit surplus labour, but rather the general reduction of the necessary labour of society to a minimum, which then corresponds to the artistic, scientific etc. development of the individuals in the time set free, and with the means created, for all of them."*

"Capital itself is the moving contradiction, [in] that it presses to reduce labour time to a minimum, while it posits labour time, on the other side, as sole measure and source of wealth. Hence it diminishes labour time in the necessary form so as to increase it in the superfluous form; hence posits the superfluous in growing measure as a condition – question of life or death – for the necessary. On the one side, then, it calls to life all the powers of science and of nature, as of social combination and of social intercourse, in order to make the creation of wealth independent (relatively) of the labour time employed on it. On the other side, it wants to use labour time as the measuring rod for the giant social forces thereby created, and to confine them within the limits required to maintain the already created value as value."

Robots and AI will only really take off when the current depressionary global economy enters a new phase. Marx noticed that *"a crisis always forms the starting-point of large new investments. Therefore, from the point of view of society as a whole ... a new material basis for the next turn-over cycle."* [184] New and massive investments will take the form of new technologies, which will be not only labour-shedding and productivity-increasing, but also new forms of domination of labour by capital.

Inasmuch as robots replace labourers, mental labour is bound to increase in importance. Given certain conditions, mental labour can be productive of value and surplus value just as objective labour. It is subject to the same rules dominating objective labour. On the one hand, new forms of mental labour allow the introduction of new forms of exploitation together with greater rates of exploitation. On the other, new technologies replace mental labourers with means of production, just as in the case of objective labour, and thus affect negatively profitability.

But perhaps the most important consequence of this analysis is that mental labour under capitalist production relations is part of today's proletariat. The proletariat is not disappearing, but is expanding with different features. In spite of its specific features, mental labour is not capitalism's elixir of life but its potential gravedigger.

The obstacle to a harmonious superabundant society based on robots reducing human toil to a minimum is Capital. As long as the means of production (and that will include robots) are owned by a few, the benefits of a robot society will accrue to the few. Whoever owns the capital will benefit as robots and AI inevitably replace many jobs. If the rewards of new technologies go largely to the very richest, then a dystopian future could become reality.

The class struggle will continue

Marx reckoned that the history of human society up to now has been the history of class struggle. Class struggle could not disappear until capitalism was replaced by common ownership and control of the means of production and social organisation by the people as a whole. This could use the technical resources to deliver a super-abundant society that would end scarcity and the need for class struggle – communism.

When Marx was writing Capital, the UK economy was experiencing a boom in profitability and growth and British capital was ruling the world and at its zenith. However, from the late 1860s, profitability turned down and the UK, along with other major economies entered a long depression through the mid-1880s (longer in the US). Depression weakened the old unions and class struggle faded. After the crushing of the Paris Commune in 1871, the first international was dispatched to retirement in New York by Marx.

If we divide the history of British capital after Marx's death in 1883, we can link the profitability of capital to the intensity of class struggle as defined by the level of strikes. In the period from the 1890s to the first world war, we find that strikes were initially high as new mass unskilled unions formed as British capital recovered some profitability after the end of the depression of 1880s. But strikes dropped off after the late 1890s as profitability reached a peak and wage demands were met. However, from the 1900s profitability of capital began to diminish and in the years leading up to the war, strong unions and a rising labour movement engaged in more intensified struggle.

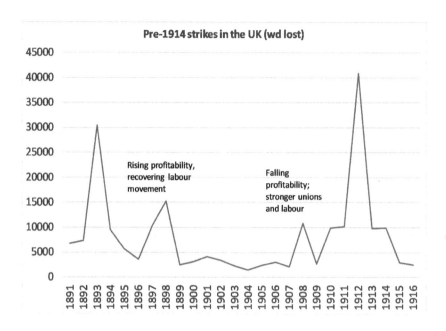

Pre-1914 strikes in the UK (wd lost)

After the end of the war that struggle resumed. But with the defeat of the transport unions in 1921 and the general strike in 1926, UK profitability jumped up and intense class struggle dropped away through to the end of the second world war.

The post-1945 period started with high profitability and growth (after 1946), leading to a recovery in trade unions (in new industries). Strikes rose a little, but class struggle was generally ameliorated by concessions and wage increases (closed shops etc). However, from the mid-1960s, UK capital entered the long profitability crisis (as in other economies). Capital needed to reverse this by crushing labour power. Strong unions took on capital in the most intense class battle since the early 1920s. Two big slumps and other neo-liberal measures defeated union power and the class struggle subsided. The neoliberal period ended in the 2000s and capitalism entered a long depression after the Great Recession. There has been no recovery in the labour movement or class struggle.

Does this mean that class struggle (the battle between capital and labour over the production of surplus value) is dead? Well, this map of the British class struggle does imply that only a recovery in profitability

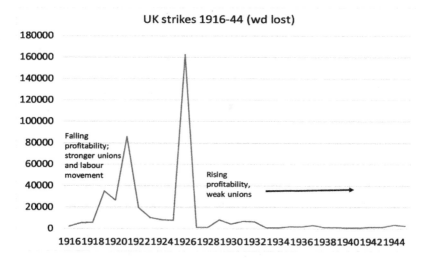

allowing labour to regain its organised strength in new industries and sectors can create the conditions for intensified struggle when profitability drops back again – as it will. That suggests a generation ahead before we can see class struggle as experienced in the 1910-26 period or in the 1970s.

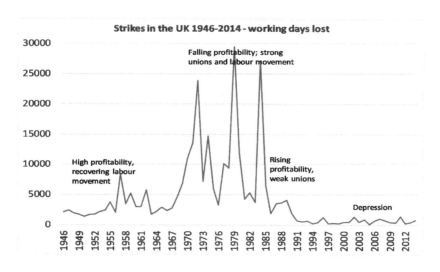

But Marx's laws about capital accumulation have not gone away. Crises will reoccur at regular intervals with the accumulation of capital and the longer capital accumulates the more difficult it will be for capital to deliver the needs and desires of humanity as capital concentrates and centralises, inequality of wealth and income remains embedded and even increases. And there is no avoidance of this downward spiral.

It is the prime result of Marx's Capital and his laws of accumulation and profitability that opposition to capitalism is not an irrational response to capitalism's temporary difficulties, but a necessity dictated by the progressive inability of the system to sustain humanity. The analysis of capitalist accumulation ends, as Marx said in a letter to Engels: *"In the class struggle as a finale in which is found the solution of the whole smear! From a struggle over wages, hours and working conditions or relief, it becomes, even as it fights for those things, a struggle for the overthrow of the capitalist system of production – a struggle for proletarian revolution."*[185]

200 years after Marx's birth

Marx was born in 1818, at the beginning of the period when capitalism started to become the dominant mode of production in Europe. His childhood was just after the end of the French revolution and the Napoleonic Wars that eventually restored monarchical rule in Europe, but also left a continual drive for democratic change as industrialisation and urbanisation spread and brought the development of a new class, the working class.

YOUNG MARX
1818-1850

Horse drawn cabs

Dark satanic mills

1848 revolution

1857 panic

Paris Commune

When Marx was a young man at university and afterwards, it was a revolutionary period. Capitalism was expanding but profitability was falling (the 'miserable forties'). Class struggle intensified with the movement of the Chartists in Britain and democratic movements in Europe that culminated in the revolutions of 1848 in which Marx and Engels participated.

After the defeat of the democratic revolutions in Europe, the period from 1850 to 1871 was one of economic boom, rising profitability and the spread of industrial capital across Europe, North America and Japan – with bourgeois politics in full control. As a mature man, Marx concentrated on developing a deeper understanding of the laws of motion of capitalism, while helping to build new international working class organisations.

The long boom came to an end just after the defeat of the first working-class state, the Paris Commune, in 1871. Profitability in the major economies had been falling from the mid-1860s, after the slump of

American civil war 1861-65

Bismarckian repression

Great Depression 1880s

1866. This prepared the way for the deep slumps of the early 1870s in various economies and the ensuing Great Depression of the 1880s and early 1890s. Marx died in the early years of this first great depression, which actually confirmed his prognosis of deep and recurring slumps in capitalist production.

Capitalism eventually recovered from the Great Depression of the 1880s and early 1890s after the sufficient devaluation of capital values through slumps. Then it entered what was called the short-lived 'belle epoque' of the 1890s and early 1900s. But rivalry between the major capitalist powers over global supremacy intensified.

One hundred years on from Marx's birth, by 1918, capitalism had become the dominant mode of production globally, but it was an uneven development with greater capitalist powers exerting control over smaller powers and over areas of the globe still to be exploited on a capitalist basis.

**BELLE EPOQUE
1890-1905**

World Fair of 1900 in Paris

Mass social democracy

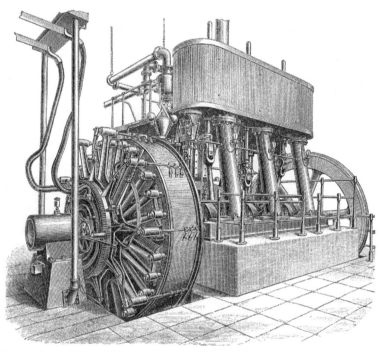

Electricity

1905 - WWI

Now cars not horses

Women's suffrage

Revolution in Russia

World War I

Imperialist rivalry had led to the first world war and also to the first wor-king-class revolution in Russia, one of the weaker and more backward capitalist states.

The defeat of revolutionary movements in Europe by the early 1920s was accompanied by short burst of economic growth and speculative investment in the 'roaring twenties'. That culminated in the 1929 crash and the Great Depression of the 1930s. Politically, there was the rise of fascism and Stalinism ending with World War 2 and the nuclear bombing of Japan. Alongside the depression was the spread of motor vehicles, commercial planes, broadcasting and other electrical appliances.

1918-46

Great Depression 1930s

Fascism

Planes

Nuclear fission and war

**1946 - 64,
THE GOLDEN AGE**

Welfare state and strong labour movement

Pax Americana

United Nations

Revolution in Portugal, Greece and Spain

International slump

Vietnam war and colonial revolution

**1982-00,
THE NEO-LIBERAL
COUNTER-REVOLUTION**

Defeat of labour militancy

Globalisation

Hi-tech revolution

After WW2, based on US capital, cheap labour in Europe and Japan, and the application of the new technologies, capitalism entered a short 'golden age' of high profitability, investment and growth. It was able to make concessions under pressure from strong labour organisations on wages and the 'social wage' of the welfare state. It was Pax America internationally as the US ruled the globe through the IMF, World Bank and the UN, while trying to weaken the Soviet states in the 'cold war'. China, however, broke free from imperialist domination with the victory of the Communists in 1946.

2000-18: THE
NEW MILLENNIUM

9/11

Falling profitability of capital in the major economies led to slower growth and the first international simultaneous slump in 1974-5. Class conflict erupted in Europe and the fascist militarist regimes of Spain, Portugal and Greece were overthrown. Anti-colonial struggle broke out with the US war in Vietnam being the pinnacle.

Banking crash and Great Recession

The slumps of 1974-5 and 1980-2 lay the economic groundwork for weakening the labour movement in Europe, the US and Japan. The strategists of capital launched what is now called 'neo-liberal' policies to take back the gains of the post-war Golden Age and restore the profitability of capital. At the same time, a new technological revolution based on computers and the internet took off.

The recovery in profitability stopped at the end of the millennium, according to Marx's law. Capitalism was 'financialised' as financial speculation replaced productive investment. This ensuing credit boom collapsed in the global financial crash of 2007-8 and the ensuing Great Recession. Internationally, US hegemony came under pressure from Islamic-inspired reaction and the 'Arab spring', particularly around the energy resources of the Middle East. The bombing and occupation of Afghanistan, Iraq and Syria was the imperialist response.

Now 200 years after Marx's birth, it seems that capitalism is in a downward trend – its ability to develop the productivity of labour and raise seven billion people out of poverty has waned. Marx's predictions of widening inequality, increased national conflict, the immiseration of labour from machines, and the destruction of natural resources, seem even more pertinent.

What will we be writing about in 2118, three hundred years from Marx's birth?

The Great Money Trick by Robert Tressell

The passage from Robert Tressell's Ragged Trousered Philanthropists, http:// libcom.org/library/ragged-trousered-philanthropists-robert-tressell *in which one of the characters cleverly outlines how the use of money under capitalism enriches capitalists and exploits the working class.*

Money is the cause of poverty because it is the device by which those who are too lazy to work are enabled to rob the workers of the fruits of their labour.'

'Prove it,' said Crass.

Owen slowly folded up the piece of newspaper he had been reading and put it into his pocket.

'All right,' he replied. 'I'll show you how the Great Money Trick is worked.'

Owen opened his dinner basket and took from it two slices of bread but as these were not sufficient, he requested that anyone who had some bread left would give it to him. They gave him several pieces, which he placed in a heap on a clean piece of paper, and, having borrowed the pocket knives they used to cut and eat their dinners with from Easton, Harlow and Philpot, he addressed them as follows:

'These pieces of bread represent the raw materials which exist naturally in and on the earth for the use of mankind; they were not made by any human being, but were created by the Great Spirit for the benefit and sustenance of all, the same as were the air and the light of the sun.'

... 'Now,' continued Owen, 'I am a capitalist; or, rather, I represent the land-lord and capitalist class. That is to say, all these raw materials belong to me. It does not matter for our present argument how I obtained possession of them, or whether I have any real right to them; the only thing that matters now is the admitted fact that all the raw materials which are necessary for the production of the necessaries of life are now the property of the Landlord and Capitalist class. I am that class: all these raw materials belong to me.'

... 'Now you three represent the Working Class: you have nothing – and for my part, although I have all these raw materials, they are of no use to me – what I need is – the things that can be made out of these raw materials by Work: but as I am too lazy to work myself, I have invented the Money Trick to make you work for me. But first I must explain that I possess something else beside the raw materials. These three knives represent – all the machinery of production; the factories, tools, railways, and so forth, without which the necessaries of life cannot be produced in abundance. And these three coins' – taking three halfpennies from his pocket – 'represent my Money Capital.'

'But before we go any further,' said Owen, interrupting himself, 'it is most important that you remember that I am not supposed to be merely "a" capitalist. I represent the whole Capitalist Class. You are not supposed to be just three workers – you represent the whole Working Class.'

... Owen proceeded to cut up one of the slices of bread into a number of little square blocks.

'These represent the things which are produced by labour, aided by machinery, from the raw materials. We will suppose that three of these blocks represent – a week's work. We will suppose that a week's work is worth – one pound: and we will suppose that each of these ha'pennies is a sovereign. ...

'Now this is the way the trick works -'

... Owen now addressed himself to the working classes as represented by Philpot, Harlow and Easton.

'You say that you are all in need of employment, and as I am the kind-hearted capitalist class I am going to invest all my money in various industries, so as to give you Plenty of Work. I shall pay each of you one pound per week, and a week's work is – you must each produce three of these square blocks. For doing this work you will each receive your wages; the money will be your own, to do as you like with, and the things you produce will of course be mine, to do as I like with. You will each take one of these machines and as soon as you have done a week's work, you shall have your money.'

The Working Classes accordingly set to work, and the Capitalist class sat down and watched them. As soon as they had finished, they passed the nine little blocks to Owen, who placed them on a piece of paper by his side and paid the workers their wages.

'These blocks represent the necessaries of life. You can't live without some of these things, but as they belong to me, you will have to buy them from me: my price for these blocks is – one pound each.'

As the working classes were in need of the necessaries of life and as they could not eat, drink or wear the useless money, they were compelled to agree to the kind Capitalist's terms. They each bought back and at once consumed one-third of the produce of their labour. The capitalist class also devoured two of the square blocks, and so the net result of the week's work was that the kind capitalist had consumed two pounds worth of the things produced by the labour of the others, and reckoning the squares at their market value of one pound each, he had more than doubled his capital, for he still possessed the three pounds in money and in addition four pounds worth of goods. As for the working classes, Philpot, Harlow and Easton, having each consumed the pound's worth of necessaries they had bought with their wages, they were again in precisely the same condition as when they started work – they had nothing.

This process was repeated several times: for each week's work the producers were paid their wages. They kept on working and spending all their earnings. The kind-hearted capitalist consumed twice as much as any one of them and his pile of wealth continually increased. In a little while – reckoning the little squares at their market value of one pound each – he was worth about one hundred pounds, and the working classes were still in the same condition as when they began, and were still tearing into their work as if their lives depended upon it.

After a while the rest of the crowd began to laugh, and their merriment increased when the kind-hearted capitalist, just after having sold a pound's worth of necessaries to each of his workers, suddenly took their tools – the Machinery of Production – the knives away from them, and informed them that as owing to Over Production all his store-houses were glutted with the necessaries of life, he had decided to close down the works.

'Well, and what the bloody 'ell are we to do now?' demanded Philpot.

'That's not my business,' replied the kind-hearted capitalist. 'I've paid you your wages, and provided you with Plenty of Work for a long time past. I have no more work for you to do at present. Come round again in a few months' time and I'll see what I can do for you.'

'But what about the necessaries of life?' demanded Harlow. 'We must have something to eat.'

'Of course you must,' replied the capitalist, affably; 'and I shall be very pleased to sell you some.'

'But we ain't got no bloody money!'

'Well, you can't expect me to give you my goods for nothing! You didn't work for me for nothing, you know. I paid you for your work and you should have saved something: you should have been thrifty like me. Look how I have got on by being thrifty!'

The unemployed looked blankly at each other, but the rest of the crowd only laughed; and then the three unemployed began to abuse the kind-hearted Capitalist, demanding that he should give them some of the necessaries of life that he had piled up in his warehouses, or to be allowed to work and produce some more for their own needs; and even threatened to take some of the things by force if he did not comply with their demands.

But the kind-hearted Capitalist told them not to be insolent, and spoke to them about honesty, and said if they were not careful he would have their faces battered in for them by the police, or if necessary he would call out the military and have them shot down like dogs.

Endnotes

1 Rolf Hecker, https://www.google.co.uk/search?q=hecker+on+1857+crisis&oq=hecker+on+1857+crisis&aqs=chrome..

2 Michael Kraetke, http://www.academia.edu/8790235/Marx_theory_or_theories_of_crisis

3 Marx-Engels, Works, Vol.33, Berlin, 1966, p.82

4 Marx to Louis Kugelmann, 13 October 1866

5 Marx to Sigfrid Meyer, 30 April 1867.

6 Karl Kautsky followed this division by presenting his *Theories of Surplus Value* as material from the fourth book and volume of *Capital*. Marx (1905–1910).

7 Marx 1987, p. 173

8 Marx to Ferdinand Lassalle, 22 February 1858.

9 Marx to Ferdinand Lassalle, 28 April 1862

10 Marx to Nikolaii Franzevich Danielson, 13 June 1871

11 Marx to Nikolaii Franzevich Danielson, 13 December 1881

12 Engels to Marx, 7 August 1865:

13 Seigel, p339 and note 26.

14 ricardo.ecn.wfu.edu/~cottrell/ope/archive/0406/att-0306/01-INTRO.DOC

15 "This is not to say that Engels never misrepresents Marx. Notoriously, he adds in his Part 3 ("The Law of the Tendential Fall in the Rate of Profit"): *"In actuality, however, the rate of profit will fall in the long run, as we have already seen"* (Marx, 1981, 337; translation modified). Even if Marx believes this, he is interested in the tendency less as a long-term law than in its interrelation with the cycle of boom and slump, as indicated by the final paragraph of Chapter 3 of the Manuscript, which Engels (also mistakenly)." in A Callinicos, Marx's unfinished but magnificent critique of political economy, Science & Society, January 2018.

16 Marx, letter to Kugelmann, 11 July 1868)

17 Capital, vol. I, p. 186

18 Robert Tressell, The Ragged Trousered Philanothropists – see epilogue.

19 Capital, vol. I, p. 39

20 Rubin.

21 Marx 1906: 86–87

22 Cockshott, W.P., and Cottrell, A., 1997a. Labour Time versus Alternative Value Bases: A research note, *Cambridge Journal of Economics*, 21, pp. 545-9. Cockshott, W.P., and Cottrell, A., 1997b. The Scientific Status of the Labour Theory of Value. In: Eastern Economic Association, *Fourth mini-conference on Value Theory*. Washington, DC, United States, April 3-6l. Available at: <http://www.wfu.edu/~cottrell/eea97.pdf>.

23 *"If the labour theory of value is correct, these ratios should be fairly narrowly distributed. Using United Kingdom input-output data we tested the candidate "value bases" oil, electricity, and iron and steel, and found correlations against price of 0.799, 0.826 and 0.576 respectively, as compared with 0.977 for labour.7 For one can focus on the ratio of aggregate price to labour-content (or alternatively labour-content to price) across the sectors of the economy."* Cockshott et al op cit.

24 http://www.anwarshaikhecon.org/sortable/images/docs/publications/political_economy/1998/1-labthvalue.pdf

25 Lefteris Tsoulfidis and Dimitris Paitaridis

26 http://gesd.free.fr/carchedi815.pdf

27 Marx Capital ch. 25, §2

28 https://www.marxists.org/archive/marx/works/1867-c1/ch24.htm#23a

29 Capital, vol. I, p. 592

30 *"The larger the Lazarus stratum of the working class and the larger the industrial reserve army, the larger too is the army of those who are officially accounted paupers. This is the absolute general law of capitalist accumulation".* Capital Vol One, Chapter 25

31 Op cit 772

32 Op cit 782-783

33 Capital Vol one p790

34 Op cit 764

35 Op cit 777.

36 http://citeseerx.ist.psu.edu/viewdoc/download?doi=10.1.1.144.4902&rep=rep1&type=pdf

37 Capital Vol 3 chapter 15

38 *"The fact that the means of production and the productivity of labour increases more rapidly than the productive population, expresses itself, therefore, capitalistically in the inverse form that the labouring population always increase more rapidly than the conditions under which capital can employ this increase for its own self-expansion".* Chapter 25

39 Grundrisse p748

40 The rise of the organic composition of capital is not the investment in an eleventh spade, when there are 10 workers and 10 spades, so that the eleventh spade is superfluous, but the replacement of the spades by equipping the men with ploughs and horses.

41 (Marx, *Capital*, Vol.1, international Publishers, New York, 1967, pp.260-261)

42 https://www.youtube.com/watch?v=-e8rt8RGjCM&app=desktop

43 David Harvey is entirely dismissive of the rising organic composition of capital as a cause of falling profitability, writing that *"it is hard to make Marx's theory of the falling rate of profit work when innovation is as much capital or means of production saving....as it is labour saving"* (Harvey, 2010: 94).

44 *"If it is said that overproduction is only relative, this is quite correct; but the entire capitalist*

mode of production is only a relative one, whose barriers are not absolute ... The contradiction of the capitalist mode of production, however, lies precisely in its tendency towards an absolute development of the productive forces, which continually come into conflict with the specific conditions of production in which capital moves, and alone can move". Vol 3 p. 366

45   Capital Volume 3 p357

46   E Maito, And yet it moves down, https://mpra.ub.uni-muenchen.de/58007/2/MPRA_paper_58007.pdf

47   Maito concludes: *"Over this long period, 1855 to 2009, two opposing trends, mediated by the interwar period, have developed, expressing the Marxian determinations explained above. The rate of accumulation reached higher levels in the post-war period (average: 3.8% per year in 1946-2009) compared to the pre-World War I period (average: 2.0% per year in 1856-1913). During these same periods, the growth in the number of employees showed the reverse, with a higher relative growth in the first part (1.3% per year) compared to post-World War II decades (0.3%). During the interwar period, in which the rate of profit recovered significantly, the accumulation rate expanded at an average annual rate of 0.5% - less than the average increase of 0.9% of the workforce."*

48   *"Since the development of the productiveness and the correspondingly higher composition of capital sets in motion an ever-increasing quantity of means of production through a constantly decreasing quantity of labour, every aliquot part of the total product i.e. every single commodity, or each particular lot of commodities in the total mass of products – absorbs less living labour, and also contains less materialised labour, both in the depreciation of the fixed capital applied and in the raw and auxiliary materials consumed. Hence every single commodity contains a smaller sum of labour materialised in means of production and of labour newly added during production. This causes the price of the individual commodity to fall. But the mass of profits contained in the individual commodities may nevertheless increase if the rate of the absolute or relative surplus value grows. The commodity contains less newly added labour, but its unpaid portion grows in relation to its paid portion. However, this is the case only within certain limits. With the absolute amount of living labour newly incorporated in individual commodities decreasing enormously as production develops, the absolute mass of unpaid labour contained in them will likewise decrease, however much it may have grown as compared to the paid portion."* www.marxists.org/archive/marx/works/1894-c3/ch13.htm. Capital Volume 3 Chapter 13.

49   "The UK rate of profit", to be published in The World in Crisis, forthcoming from Haymarket Books, 2018

50   In the 1930s, however: *"In terms of the balance of class forces, while labour was severely weakened by mass unemployment, capital could not take advantage because of the collapse in world markets. The comfortable corporatism engendered by the shelter of protectionist tariffs was not a period of intense class struggle. Indeed, for capital, the adverse effects of a return to gold at an overvalued exchange rate and the collapse of the international economy into a protectionist, semi-autarky just about counterbalanced the positive effects of the General Strike victory and the rapid rise of unemployment. Apart then from the first half of the 1920s, the rise in the rate of profit did not have as a contributory factor a rise in the rate of surplus-value. Rather, the rate of profit was driven up by the maintenance of productivity growth while capital intensity fell."* Brown and Mohun, http://gesd.free.fr/mohun11.pdf

51   As Marx said in his notes for Capital, historically it was known by the classical economists that the rate of profit on capital tended to fall, but they had no explanation. Marx's laws of value and accumulation provide the theoretical answer: *"The transformation of surplus value into profit is to be derived out of the transformation of the rate of surplus value into the rate of profit, not vice versa. And in fact, it is the rate of profit where one starts from historically.*

Surplus value and rate of surplus value are relative, invisible and the essential to be investigated, while the rate of profit and hence the surplus value in the form of profit show on the surface of what appears." In the manuscript of the third volume in MEGA2 II 4.2, p. 52.

52 Karl Marx, Marx Engels Collected Works, vol. 33 (London: Lawrence and Wishart, 1990), 104; Karl Marx, The Grundrisse (London: Penguin, 1973), p. 748.

53 Marx 1973, pp. 748-49, emphasis added.

54 "*In light of the fact that 'the principal laws governing crises' are, as all social laws, tendential and contradictory, 'to determine mathematically' the laws is an impossible task. First, mathematics is a branch of formal logic. As seen above, premises in formal logic cannot be contradictory. However, to account for the laws of movement in society one has to start from contradictory premises and this is why the laws of movement are tendential. Second, even if all the 'factors involved' were known, it would be practically impossible to consider all of them. This is why econometric models, even large ones involving thousands of relations, have such a dismal record as tools of prediction. But if it is impossible to determine the laws of crises purely in terms of mathematics, it is certainly possible to analyse the cyclical movement of economic indicators (the ups and downs) by using 'higher mathematics'. This was Marx's intuition.*" G. Carchedi, *Behind the Crisis* (Leiden: Brill, 2011).

55 C. Harman, "The Rate of Profit and the World Today," *International Socialism* 115 (2007); available at http://isj.org.uk/the-rate-of-profit-and-the-world-today/

56 This holds per unit of capital invested. Total employment depends also on capital accumulation.

57 For a fuller analysis of Marx's law and a defense of the critical arguments against it, see G. Carchedi and M. Roberts, "Old and New Misconceptions of Marx's Law," *Critique: Journal of Socialist Theory* 41 (2014), 571–94.

58 "*The periodical depreciation of existing capital—one of the means immanent in capitalist production to check the fall of the rate of profit and hasten accumulation of capital—value through formation of new capital—disturbs the given conditions, within which the process of circulation and reproduction of capital takes place, and is therefore accompanied by sudden stoppages and crises in the production process.*" Marx, *Capital*, vol. 3, chapter 15.

59 Marx Grundrisse 1968 512

60 Marx, CW32, 157-8.

61 https://en.wikipedia.org/wiki/Tulip_mania

62 "*The theory of crises most fully (though far from completely) developed in the 1864–65 Manuscript, and already sketched out in earlier drafts, posits an interaction between the tendency of the rate of profit to fall and the cycle of bubble and panic on financial markets, which feeds the accumulation of capital in good times and accomplishes in bad times the destruction of capital required to restore profitability*" A Callinicos, Deciphering Capital, 2014, ch. 6.

63 Capital Volume 3 p359

64 Capital Volume 3 p572

65 Capital Volume 3 p 621

66 Kraetke op cit.

67 in his seminal work, *Economic crisis and crisis theory*

68 Economic Crisis and Crisis Theory. Paul Mattick 1974, https://www.marxists.org/archive/mattick-paul/1974/crisis/ch02.htm

69 G Carchedi, The Return from the Grave, 2009

70 *"The basic point is that financial crises are caused by the shrinking productive base of the economy. A point is thus reached at which there has to be a sudden and massive deflation in the financial and speculative sectors. Even though it looks as though the crisis has been generated in these sectors, the ultimate cause resides in the productive sphere and the attendant falling rate of profit in this sphere."* Carchedi, <u>Behind the Crisis.</u>

71 Maito op cit

72 Karl Marx to Friedrich Engels, 1865

73 CI, 633

74 (31.05.73, CW44, 504).

75 (CW29, 105)

76 (CIII, 477n).

77 https://en.wikipedia.org/wiki/Cl%C3%A9ment_Juglar

78 Pavel Maksakovsky, The Capitalist Cycle, Haymarket 2009.

79 Kliman, The failure of capitalist production, 2012.

80 G Carchedi, Frontiers of Political Economy. http://digamo.free.fr/carchedi91.pdf.

81 H Grossman, The law of accumulation, Pluto Press 1992

82 Kliman op cit chap 8.

83 See David Harvey, https://thenextrecession.wordpress.com/2014/12/17/david-harvey-monomaniacs-and-the-rate-of-profit/

84 Dispatches for the New York Tribune, Penguin p201.

85 Marx Theories of Surplus Value, Volume 2. p. 514.

86 https://thenextrecession.wordpress.com/2016/08/09/the-great-financial-meltdown/

87 In a report to clients (*The convulsions of political economy*, 16 August 2011), Magnus kicks off by quoting Marx's *Preface to a contribution to the critique of political economy*, written in 1859.

88 Capital Volume 2, note

89 *Mistaken Marxist moments*, FT, 26 August 2011).

90 With time on his hands at the Californian Democratic Convention, he decided to (re-read) Marx's *Theories of Surplus Value*, or at least Chapter 17

91 (*http://www.nytimes.com/roomfordebate/2014/03/30/was-marx-right*).

92 https://en.wikipedia.org/wiki/Immiseration_thesis

93 Capitalism: 50 ideas you really need to know. Some of the points in that book were repeated up in Portes' article in the centre-left British journal, The New Statesman, entitled 'What Marx got right'.

94 Marxist economist Simon Mohun has shown that less than 2% of income earners in the US fit that bill. https://thenextrecession.files.wordpress.com/2015/09/classstructure-1918to2011wmf.pdf

95 T Piketty, Capital in the 21st century.

96 Keynesian Paul Samuelson

97 Paul A. Samuelson's "Understanding the Marxian Notion of Exploitation: A Summary of the So-called Transformation Problem between Marxian Values and Competitive Prices, "J. Econ. Lit., June 1971, 9 (2), pp. 399-431).

98 Eugene Bohm-Bawerk tried to do that in the late 1890s,

99 Keynes, Laissez-Faire and Communism, 1926

100 Paul Samuelson, The transformation of values: what Marx really meant.

101 "Every child knows that any nation that stopped working, not for a year, but let us say, just for a few weeks, would perish.... This constitutes the economic laws of all societies, including capitalism. And every child knows, too, that the amounts of products corresponding to the differing amounts of needs, demand differing and quantitatively determined amounts of society's aggregate labour", Letter from Marx to Kugelmann, 11 July 1868, MECW, vol.43, pp.68-69.

102 Carchedi, Yaffe, Kliman, Freeman

103 Fred Moseley, Money and Totality

104 Moseley op cit p229

105 Carchedi has shown that the money price average rate of profit is close to the value average rate of profit (i.e. across a whole economy).

106 Total value is pretty close to total prices measured in money terms

107 Let Marx speak for himself. "In Capital-Profit, or better Capital-Interest, Land-Rent, Labour-Wages of Labour, in this economic trinity expressing professedly the connection of value and of wealth in general with their sources, we have the complete mystification of the capitalist mode of production. ... This formula corresponds at the same time to the interests of the ruling classes, by proclaiming the natural necessity and eternal justification of their sources of revenue and raising them to the position of a dogma." (Volume III, Chapter 48, pp. 966-67).

108 Sraffa

109 Joan Robinson

110 Michal Kalecki

111 James Steuart, the classical economist

112 https://en.wikipedia.org/wiki/Accumulation_by_dispossession

113 http://www.tandfonline.com/doi/pdf/10.1080/13604813.2013.853865

114 https://www.amazon.co.uk/Readers-Guide-Marxs-Capital/dp/1910885487

115 Promoted prominently by Costas Lapavitsas and Jack Rasmus,

116 I have discussed the theories of Costas Lapavitsas and Rasmus before and see Tony Norfield's insightful critique of Lapavitsas' approach. And see Sam Williams in his blog

Endnotes

117 https://critiqueofcrisistheory.wordpress.com/

118 https://en.wikipedia.org/wiki/Capital_in_the_Twenty-First_Century

119 Esteban Ezequiel Maito, The historical transience of capital, the downward trend in the rate of profit since the 19th century, University of Buenos Aires, for evaluation, https://uba.academia.edu/EstebanMaito

120 Keynes op cit

121 Marx, 22 MECW, vol.48, p.136

122 See the excellent book by Nicholas Wapshott, *Keynes/Hayek*

123 Ibid: 186

124 In his 1978 book: "Factors in Business Investment," published by the NBER, Bob Eisner summarized much of his work on investment. The opening paragraph of the book's introduction captures well why investment is bound to be a perennial topic in economics: "*Few economists or business analysts need be reminded of the importance of investment. First, investment contributes to future output; net investment to economic growth. Second, it contributes to current demand and current employment. Understandably, there is much sentiment for encouraging investment, or at least for removing discouraging influences, to permit these contributions to be optimal.*"

125 John Maynard Keynes, "Proposals for a Revenue Tariff," The New Statesman and Nation (March 7, 1931), reprinted in Essays in Persuasion.

126 JM Keynes, Collected Writings, Vol 13, P343.

127 Minsky, H. P. 1991. The financial instability hypothesis: A clarification. In The risk of economic crisis. M. Feldstein, ed., Chicago: University of Chicago Press, pp. 158-166.

128 James Montier, http://www.zerohedge.com/sites/default/files/images/user5/imageroot/2012/02/Montier%20-%20What%20goes%20up%20must%20come%20down.pdf

129 Where profits come from, 2008.

130 José A. Tapia, 'Investment, profits, and crises — Theories and evidence', chapter in World in Crisis, eds G Carchedi and Michael Roberts, Zero Books, forthcoming 2017.

131 Minsky op cit

132 JM Keynes, The General Theory, Chapter 22.

133 P Mattick, Economic crisis and crisis theory, 1974. https://www.marxists.org/archive/mattick-paul/1974/crisis/ch01.htm

134 This idea was first mooted to me by Andrew Kliman in email discussions.

135 The behavior of aggregate corporate investment, August 2015, AggregateInvestment

136 G Carchedi, M Roberts The Long Roots Of The Present Crisis: Keynesians, Austerians, And Marx's Law, Chapter One, In World In Crisis, (forthcoming Haymarket Books, 2018)

137 JP Morgan, Profit stall threatens global expansion, Special Report, 21 June 2016

138 ec 201609 recession probabilities

139 http://www.zerohedge.com/news/2016-06-04/when-will-recession-start-deutsche-banks-disturbing-answer

140   Data come from the Federal Reserve's seasonally-adjusted Flow of Funds accounts. Shaded regions indicate NBER recessions

141   Carchedi and Roberts, The Long Roots of the present crisis, http://gesd.free.fr/rob-carch13.pdf .

142   Granger causation regression analysis show that the correlation between profits and investment was 0.43 with least squares regression coefficient at 0.60. Profits 'Granger caused' investment with a one-year lag. And investment 'Granger caused' GDP with a two-year lag. But there was no causal connection from investment to profits – the same result as Tapia. This regression analysis used annual data on GDP, profits and investment for the US from 1961 to 2014. This analysis and results can be found here. https://thenextrecession.files.wordpress.com/2017/04/profits-investment-gdp-us-1960-2014.xlsx

143   Carchedi , The old is dying but the new cannot be born: on the exhaustion of Western capitalism, in World in Crisis, op cit.

144   J Tapia: Profits encourage investment, investment dampens profits, and government spending has little effect — Business-cycle dynamics in the US, 1929-2013, unpublished, *"Thus on the basis of the results of the analysis it can be said with confidence that profits stimulate investment and that investment cuts future profits. However, on the basis of the analysis not much can be said on the relation between government spending and investment."*

145   G Carchedi, op cit

146   Rethinking Economics

147   ugly importance of rising inequality

148   In the Long Run We are all Dead

149   Branco Milanovic has done major work on measuring inequality of income per head between countries and regions

150   https://en.wikipedia.org/wiki/Kuznets_curve

151   CHINA PAPER July 2015

152   Capital, Chapter 15

153   https://www.marxists.org/archive/lenin/works/1916/imp-hsc/

154   https://www.marxists.org/archive/grossman/1929/breakdown/

155   https://www.haymarketbooks.org/books/693-the-long-depression

156   http://www.nordregio.se/en/Metameny/About-Nordregio/Journal-of-Nordregio/2008/Journal-of-Nordregio-no-1-2008/The-Three-Waves-of-Globalisation/

157   https://www.mckinsey.com/global-themes/employment-and-growth/debt-and-not-much-deleveraging

158   https://arxiv.org/PS_cache/arxiv/pdf/1107/1107.5728v2.pdf

159   CPB World Trade Monitor, November 2016, http://www.cpb.nl/en/figure/cpb-world-trade-monitor-november-2016

160   IMF World Economic Outlook, October 2016, http://www.imf.org/external/pubs/ft/weo/2016/02/

161 *Turbulence ahead: Renewing consensus amidst greater volatility, McKinsey Global Institute, September 2016*

162 Deutsche Bank, Long-Term Asset Return Study, strategists Jim Reid, Nick Burns, and Sukanto Chanda, http://uk.businessinsider.com/deutsche-bank-on-the-end-of-an-economic-era-2016-9?r=US&IR=T

163 John Smith, Imperialism in the Twenty-First Century: Globalization, Super-Exploitation, and Capitalism's Final Crisis, Monthly Review Press, 2016

164 . http://blogs.ft.com/the-exchange/2016/11/15/how-far-will-the-pendulum-swing-against-globalisation.

165 UN World Population Prospects, 2015 Revision, http://esa.un.org/unpd/wpp/Publications/Files/Key_Findings_WPP_2015.pdf.

166 Global Trends: The Paradox of Progress,

167 Engels, https://www.marxists.org/archive/marx/works/1877/anti-duhring/index.htm

168 *http://deepblue.lib.umich.edu/bitstream/handle/2027.42/93589/Tapia&Carpintero_Dynamics_of_climate_change.pdf?sequence=1*

169 Grundrisse p567-568

170 Capital, pp. 537-8.

171 https://www.oxfordmartin.ox.ac.uk/downloads/academic/The_Future_of_Employment.pdf

172 https://www.weforum.org/agenda/2017/06/the-future-is-automated-but-what-does-that-really-mean-for-jobs

173 https://www2.deloitte.com/content/dam/Deloitte/uk/Documents/finance/deloitte-uk-technology-and-people.pdf

174 http://www.slate.com/articles/business/the_dismal_science/1997/01/the_accidental_theorist.html

175 http://cep.lse.ac.uk/pubs/download/dp1461.pdf

176 http://faculty.econ.ucdavis.edu/faculty/gclark/papers/wage%20-%20jpe%20-2004.pdf

177 http://www.ggdc.net/Maddison/other_books/HS-8_2003.pdf

178 Dmitriev, V. K., 1974. Economic essays on value, competition and utility. Cambridge University Press, London, originally published between 1898–1902, Moscow

179 https://www.penguin.co.uk/books/188551/postcapitalism/

180 *http://thenewobjectivity.com/pdf/marx.pdf).*

181 Engels, Socialism: utopian and scientific

182 For more on this, see G Carchedi's Behind the Crisis, pp 225-232 (http://digamo.free.fr/carched11.pdf).

183 https://www.marxists.org/archive/marx/works/1857/grundrisse/ch14.htm

184 Marx, Capital Vol. II, p.186

185 Marx to Engels, quoted from Mattick https://www.marxists.org/archive/mattick-paul/1955/keynes.htm